The Youth and Teen Running Encyclopedia

A Complete Guide for Middle and Long Distance Runners
Ages 6 to 18

Mick Grant and John Molvar

Coaches at Youth Runner Magazine

Youth Guide to
Better Middle and Long Distance Running

Cover Photo:
Russell Brown winning the 2011 New Balance Indoor Grand Prix Mile, over 2 Olympic medalists and the American Mile Record Holder. Russell's youth coach was Mick Grant
Courtesy photo, **Victah Sailer, photorun.net**

Page 1 Photo:
Russell Brown, at age 14, winning the 1999 Hershey's National Final in the 800
Courtesy photo, **Property of The Hershey Company**

ISBN-13   978-1495425783
ISBN-10   1495425789

Table of Contents

A: FOREWORD

Mick Grant has been coaching youth athletes for over 30 years with astonishing success. Parents of many ordinary local kids have requested him to coach their children to become better runners. Mick rarely recruited athletes; they came to him and most had minimal or no background in the sport before starting with him. The results he has gotten are nothing short of remarkable including National Champions six consecutive years and having qualified athletes for the Hershey National Championships 12 years in a row. Several of his runners have gone on to become State and National high school champions including Russell Brown, who went on to run a 3:51 mile and Chantelle Dron, who ran a 4:22 1500 meter run at age 15. The accomplishments of some of his athletes are highlighted throughout the book.

How could one coach have this much success? A cynic would assume he is a taskmaster who works these kids to near death. Nothing can be further than the truth. In fact, Mick, as this book details, uses a **FUN FIRST** approach to training. He makes sure the athlete is, first and foremost, enjoying what they are doing. His coaching methods are based on intelligent, moderate but consistent and gradual progression towards improvement with emphasis on preventing injuries and illness. He also individually tailors his training for each athlete, factoring in age, background in running if any, health and, most importantly, ensuring that the athlete is enjoying what they are doing.

One of the most important measures of a coach is what happens when a runner moves on. Are the kids burned out and tired of running or do they enjoy the sport and wish to continue onward to higher success? On that score, Mick's record is outstanding as most of his athletes move on with a love of running and a thirst for more. Mick's kids have gone on to run at many fine schools including Harvard, Princeton, Stanford, Dartmouth, Haverford College, Cornell, Colorado State, Colgate, Boston University, Boston College, Yale, University of New Hampshire, UNC Charlotte, NYU, RPI, Bates, Amherst, UMass Lowell and others. Mick has also been a frequent and long time contributor to Youth Runner Magazine/Youthrunner.com. We highly recommend you use this resource which is detailed in Chapter 40. This book is a must read for youth runners age 6 to 18 and anyone helping youth runners starting on the way to a lifelong enjoyment of running and successful running career including youth runners, parents of youth runners, youth runner club coaches and high school coaches. While this book is geared to youth runners, it is a valuable resource to all middle and distance runners and coaches regardless of age or level because the same basic principles apply to all middle and distances runners.

Follow Mick Grant on Twitter at @FunFirstCoach

Foreword by John Molvar, UMass Lowell, Assistant Coach
Prior: Gordon College, Head Coach, Track & Field and Cross Country

 Courtesy photo, John Molvar

John Molvar is also the author of the book;
Fundamental Stock Investing and Wealth Building
www.amazon.com/dp/B00HZ3PZ00

Photo: Chantelle Dron, who Mick Grant coached to a 4:22 1500 (worth a 4:43 mile) at age 15. She also was a 2 time Footlocker Finalist. Courtesy photo, Cheryl Treworgy/ prettysporty.com

B.   INTRODUCTION AND CORE BELIEFS

I am grateful for the opportunity to coach young athletes. It is an honor to have worked with many of my kids for several years. I also have enjoyed working with Youth Runner Magazine (www.youthrunner.com) over the years, helping many young athletes, as well as their parents and coaches. In all my years coaching, the main question I get is, "What can I do to get better?" It is a tricky question, since every athlete is an individual and has a unique athletic background. It is important to start at the beginning and make progress patiently and consistently. Never take shortcuts. We will work through many topics involved in becoming a better middle and long distance runner.

- **The key to success in coaching is doing the right thing for the right reason.**

I've had the pleasure and privilege to speak with some of the best coaches in the world and I have read the works of many others. Coaches must be students of the sport and must always be eager to learn more. When a young, dedicated athlete gives a coach the opportunity to help them develop as an athlete, it requires a 100% commitment from the coach. I enjoy working with the kids and helping them to improve. If I do a good job, my athletes are learning a good system on how to train properly. Hopefully, we have laid a good foundation for our kids, one on which they can build a fun and successful running career. This is what we believe in, and everything we will put forward in this book is based on our opinion and experience of what works best for our kids.

1. FUN FIRST

FUN FIRST is the overriding principle throughout this book. In general, if it isn't fun, don't do it. Distance running is not supposed to be punishment; it should be, and needs to be fun. Running is a healthy form of exercise, and should be part of a lifelong healthy lifestyle. We have two main rules;

1. **Have Fun**
2. **Stay Healthy (i.e. avoid injuries and illness)**

What we want to accomplish is to make practice fun and keep the kids healthy so there are no unplanned days off. We want to steadily increase endurance and improve basic speed while making training rewarding and enjoyable. Whether the athlete is 10 years old and runs three days per week, or 18 years old and running seven days per week, a goal is that zero days are missed in training due to injury or illness.

We are not going to suggest, nor do we believe, that young athletes should participate in only one sport or activity. In fact, we encourage kids to try lots of different sports and activities in addition to running to discover what they really love. Running should be just a part of a young person's life. It is a great sport in many ways. Running relieves stress, plus kids can actually talk to their friends through about 90% of every practice! In addition, if you follow the guidelines of this book, proper training requires a much lower time commitment than any other sport. Developing endurance and speed is an important part of most sports, so running will supplement other sports they are interested in. As children grow up, they can begin the process of narrowing their focus to the things they really love.

When we talk about **FUN FIRST**, we don't suggest that our athletes goof off and don't work hard. They definitely work. The trick is to make work fun, so the kids enjoy coming to practice.

Part of having fun is discovering one's limits and pushing these limits. It is accepting the challenge to improve. This will require the athlete to push themselves a little, but it is very rewarding. It is fun to accept the challenge and rise to this challenge. You could say that the more you improve, the more fun you will have!

2.   OUR PHILOSOPY

Part of coaching is allowing an athlete's ability to reveal itself. As coaches, we should have a plan, observe and adjust. I think there are two main coaching styles; one which allows talent to emerge and one which prevents talent from emerging. Every young athlete is a diamond in the rough. As legendary coach Arthur Lydiard said, there are champions in every neighborhood. Even kids with little apparent natural ability can progress astonishingly far with intelligent and consistent training.

In training, our kids are on a long term development plan. This is what differentiates our coaching philosophy from most coaches and most other books. Everything we do is geared to making the athlete much better next year than they are now by a unique combination of constantly building endurance and improving basic speed. That means helping athletes develop over time so they run in high school, college and beyond. This is why most of Mick's athletes developed good range from 800 through cross country race distances. We try to do the right things for the right reasons. We believe in leaving room for training development. We must be able to, **always**, do more this year than we did last year. The most important thing we do is oversee recovery. Are our athletes recovering, adapting and improving from their work?

We don't race just because there is a race on the calendar. We believe that each race should be aimed at a specific objective; we don't believe in running lots of meaningless races. We want young middle distance athletes to develop good range, so we work on improving at every running event from 200 meters through 800 meters.

Photo: Mick Grant's future middle distance runners ecstatic after qualifying for the 4 x 100 relay at the Hershey Nationals.
Courtesy photo, Ken Stejbach, Seacoast Online

Photo: Katie Dlesk who Mick Grant coached to Hershey's Massachusetts State 100 title and was also a Hershey National Finalist in the 100. At Philips Academy she set numerous records and later went on to be captain of the Yale track team.
Courtesy photo,
Cheryl Treworgy,
prettysporty.com

We don't like our kids to run the 1500 meters or mile on the track until they have become good 800m runners. We like to learn how to race fast while developing endurance. We want our kids to develop very good endurance before running the mile, so let's get good 400m and 800m starting points before beginning a high school career. We have had multiple National Champions in both the 800 meters and the 4 x 800 meter relay, so this system has worked for our kids.

Remember that even though we are working on improving our basic speed in shorter events, we are primarily putting in mileage to build endurance. Working on both basic speed and endurance are the key components for long term success in middle distance running. Building endurance is like putting money in the bank, so most of our practice time is spent in endurance training. We limit anaerobic interval training to brief periods prior to target races. As kids gain experience and physical maturity, the speed and endurance components will come together. We will now move on to teaching parents, coaches and athletes our training system.

Photo of Mick Grant's Lynx Elite Junior Olympics National Champion 4 x 800 relay team which ran 7:41.10. (L-R: Russell Brown, Phil Shaw, Michael Grant, Harry Norton) Brown was a multiple youth individual and relay National champion, New England high school track champion in the 600 and eventually ran 3:51 for the mile. Shaw ran a 4:14 mile in high school, Norton was a New England Private school champion and ran a 4:14 mile in high school and 4:02 in college. Grant was a Massachusetts State Class mile champion.
Courtesy photo, Lynx Elite Athletics/Giles Norton

Photo: Marian Bihrle was coached by Mick Grant. Bihrle later became a Massachusetts State Indoor Mile champion. Later in college at Princeton she ran a 9:36 3000 and was a qualifier for the NCAA XC Championships.
Courtesy photo, Lynx Elite Athletics/Giles Norton

3. THE ROLE OF THE COACH

DEVELOPMENT 101

- **Developing as a young runner should be simple.**
- **Start at the bottom and "Climb the Ladder" one step at a time.**
- **The goal over time is your own gradual improvement.**
- **Fun + Motivation + Direction + Work + Consistency are key to long term Success**

Coaches should set the direction for athletes to go and then adjust as the situation dictates. It is critical to observe and make adjustments. A rigid training plan is more likely to result in breakdowns such as illness or injury. Do not blindly follow a rigid training plan if the athlete is not responding positively to the training. A coach should involve his athlete in developing a training plan. For example, if the coach wants an athlete to run the mile and the athlete wants to run 400 meters, there is a potential problem that needs to be worked through. I think it is a better long term strategy to keep athletes motivated in events they are excited about.

A long term plan can still include "moving the athlete up" to a longer event as endurance and confidence improve, but it is not a good idea to force things. We feel that, even if a youth athlete is racing at 400m, he should be primarily in endurance training most of the time. Endurance should be the primary focus of coaches in every middle distance and long distance event. We also believe all middle and distance athletes should be working to improve basic speed most of the year. This is an area that is almost universally neglected by middle distance and distance coaches. We are not talking about anaerobic interval training that most coach's favor; we are talking about improving basic speed which will be explained later in the book.

- **Remember, the coach is there for the athlete, not vice versa.**

C. TRAINING

Virtually every practice begins like this;
Athlete: "What are we doing today?"
Coach: "I thought we'd go for a run."

4. ENDURANCE TRAINING

"PUT MONEY IN THE BANK"

Be sure to have medical clearance from your doctor before ever beginning an exercise program.

- "It is better to under-train than to over-train." - Bill Bowerman
- Know what you can handle -- and do that -- start someplace.
- Run an amount that you enjoy. Have fun.
- Training pace doesn't matter much for beginners; pace will get faster over time.
- Run at a pace which will allow you to carry on a conversation.
- As you get stronger, increase the distance gradually.
- As you get stronger, your training pace will gradually get faster.
- Over time, incorporate a variety of training paces into your plan.

The key to success at any distance from 800 meters up is endurance. What we are trying to develop with endurance training is improved aerobic capability. We can improve endurance in a young athlete for year after year after year. While anaerobic interval training is necessary to peak for a target race, gains are only temporary. The foundation of the *FUN FIRST* program is to continue to build endurance year after year. Without getting too scientific, some of what we want to improve, and will cover, in this section include;

- **Development of the heart muscle** We want more blood pumped through the body with each beat.
- **Increase muscle capillarization** We want to deliver as much oxygen as possible to muscles.
- **Increase Aerobic Threshold** We want to run faster aerobically and for a longer period of time.

- **Improving Basic Speed** Regardless of genetic potential, all runners can improve their basic speed.
- **Increase Stride Rate** We want more strides per minute. (Goal 180+)
- **Increase Stride Length** We want to cover more ground with each stride through strength gains. We also want to avoid and eliminate any over striding. **It is very important to do this correctly.**

Training theory boiled down is very simple. As wise coaches are well aware, you are either putting money in the bank or you are taking it out. Aerobic distance running puts money in the bank. Racing and anaerobic interval training takes money out of the bank. Spend hard earned money wisely. The responsibility of the coach is to teach the athlete how to safely put lots of money in the bank and the appropriate time to spend it. The "Money in the Bank" analogy really sums up endurance training. I learned it from my friend, Buddy Bostick.

5. KEEPING A TRAINING LOG
BLACK DAYS AND RED DAYS

We recommend keeping a training journal, to record all information regarding training and racing. A training log is critical for the athlete and coach to record and periodically review to track progress over time and to identify what worked and what didn't. What we strongly suggest for a format is keeping "**Black Days**" and "**Red Days**." Black Days include all aerobic running, the vast majority of training, and are written into the training journal in **BLACK**. **Red Days** include all races and anaerobic workouts and are written into the training journal in **RED**. The number of **Red Days** should rarely exceed 10% of total training volume. Too many **Red Days** will sacrifice long term gain for short term results. At least 90% of all mileage should be **BLACK DAYS**, for better long term development. If you ever look at your training journal and see that it has become bright red, there may be trouble ahead. Every **Red Day** is money coming out of the bank. We want our young athletes to be working on building a strong aerobic endurance foundation.
If we keep taking money out of the bank, we'll end up broke. The responsibility of the coach is to teach the athlete how to safely put lots of money in the bank and the appropriate time to spend it.

Best advice - *Put money into the bank.*

Above Photo: Some of Mick's athletes with Arthur Lydiard.
Courtesy photo, Emily Raymond

6. THE INFLUENCE OF ARTHUR LYDIARD

Our training principles owe a huge debt to the legendary Arthur Lydiard, the father of modern middle/long distance training. Because all successful coaches use many of his principles we believe it is important to recognize his contribution at this point in the book. **Here is a brief summary of Lydiard's training principles.**

1) LYDIARD BELIEVED THAT THERE ARE CHAMPIONS IN EVERY NEIGHBORHOOD

Lydiard trained a bunch of kids in his neighborhood and many of them became national champions and record setters; even Olympic Champions and World Record Breakers!

2) ENDURANCE IS THE KEY TO ANY RACE 800 AND UP

The most important part of training is first building an endurance (aerobic) base. Without it, you will not reach your potential no matter what else you do. We believe very young beginning kids must do only what is fun.

3) BALANCE ENDURANCE TRAINING WITH INTERVAL TRAINING

You need the correct blend of both aerobic distance running and anaerobic interval training to race at your best. If you do one without the other, you will not achieve optimal results. An aerobic base is the "cake" and anaerobic work is the "frosting". We recommend 90% of annual training should be aerobic development. Athletes 12 and under should not do any anaerobic interval training.

4) BUILD AN ENDURANCE BASE FIRST

This is the most important phase of training. Do it for as many weeks as possible. Don't run too slow (jog) and don't run too fast (race). Do run at a strong pace. You should feel like you could have gone faster if you had to and you should feel pleasantly tired after each run.

5) VARY YOUR DISTANCES DURING THE ENDURANCE BASE PHASE

Alternate shorter runs and longer runs. Do a long run once a week. Do shorter, faster tempo runs once or twice a week.

6) DO A HILL PHASE

Lydiard believed a few weeks of hill running will transition you, or get you ready for the intervals you will be doing in the next phase.

7) ANAEROBIC PHASE

Do four or five weeks of anaerobic interval training to condition your body to learn race pace and handle the lactic acid you will feel in the race when you tire. Don't overdo it. Train, don't strain, and stop when you feel you have had enough for a day. Goal times and number of intervals is just a guide. Don't carry this phase on too many weeks or you will break down.

8) WORK ON BASIC SPEED

Do repeat short sprints of 40 to 200 meters to improve basic speed. Our natural sprint speed is somewhat determined by genetics but everyone can improve their speed. Focus on running tall, high knee lift, and relaxation. We believe the athlete should be working on basic speed most of the year.

9) CO-ORDINATION PHASE TRAINING

Coordinate or bring together aerobic endurance training and anaerobic interval training by running developmental races or time trials. These are early season, unimportant races that you are basically just using for training.

10) TAPER FOR THE TARGET RACE

The last 7 to 10 days before your target race, back off training by about 25% so you are rested and fresh.

Arthur Lydiard is the single most influential distance coach in history. His methods are used in one form or another by most coaches around the world. He is also very controversial, in that his mantra of high mileage is sometimes intimidating and misunderstood. He is the icon

of distance running. A distance based coaching philosophy, which includes long runs, is widely considered a form of the Lydiard System.

Arthur Lydiard and Coach Mick
Courtesy photo, Emily Raymond

There can be little doubt that an athlete who runs 20 miles per week will likely be a fitter runner than one who doesn't run at all. By the same token, an elite athlete who eventually builds up to Lydiard's recommended 100 miles per week will likely be much fitter than one who runs 20 miles per week. Lydiard preached that the ideal goal for an elite athlete is to run 100 aerobic miles per week, which was based on 30 years of trial and error on himself. His goal was to build as much endurance as possible through distance running in the aerobic range for as long as possible and use interval training to get race sharpened for a specific race.

Although we will miss Arthur Lydiard, his message will be around, and argued, used and misused forever. Arthur Lydiard was a treasure, and he has left us with a lot. On December 12, 2004, Arthur Lydiard passed away at the age of 87.

Lydiard with Mick's athletes **Courtesy photo, Emily Raymond**

7.   PERIODIZATION
BREAKING THE YEAR INTO BLOCKS

    Periodization is a widely used method of planned training to be ready for specific races. The year is broken into blocks or phases, each of which concentrates on specific aspects of training. The goals of the runner will dictate the timing and the length of the different phases in their training. The goals of different runners vary widely, from the runner who only really cares about one target race a year, to the youth runner trying to peak twice a year (XC in the fall and track in the summer), to the high school or college runner who is trying to peak 3 seasons each year (XC in the fall, indoor track in the winter and outdoor track in the spring), to the road racer who wants to run in 30-40 races throughout the year and try to be fairly competitive in most of them. Our periodized year starts with a **Base Phase** where the focus is on building aerobic endurance and improving basic speed. This is followed by an **Anaerobic Phase** where interval training is used to develop lactic acid tolerance. Next is a **Race Phase** which includes early season races followed by a tapering period just before the target race of the season. After the final race, there is a brief **End of Season Recovery Phase**. Often the end of the Anaerobic Phase will overlap with the beginning of the Race Phase.

Our athletes will spend most of their year in Base Phase endurance training and basic speed improvement. This is because our main goal is for the runner to be much better next year than they are this year. This is where our system and this book differ from most other books and training systems. After a couple of years in our system, we want our athletes to be way ahead of similarly talented kids in their age group. We also want to build a big aerobic foundation for long term success. This is much more important than running lots and lots of races. We might have ten months or more of endurance training including daily distance runs and high aerobic tempo runs. We will also work on improving basic speed during this time. We typically spend only one month on anaerobic interval training and one month of racing. The main difference between this book and many other training books is that we are looking specifically at developing young athletes for long term improvement, not short-sighted goals. We spend much more time helping young athletes build a good foundation, to help prepare the young athlete for future success and maybe to eventually become an elite athlete.

Spend more time on aerobic training, for long term improvement, and less time on interval based anaerobic training, which produces short term peaking.

The ideal for the youth runner is to periodize their schedule to be ready to peak for two primary target races, one track race in the spring/summer and one cross country race in the fall. Use little or no anaerobic interval training in the fall. That season should be almost entirely aerobic endurance base phase training. We do not mean to say that running fast is not important. Developing basic speed as much as possible is critical. Work on basic speed (as explained later in the book) most of the year, but limit the stressful lactic acid accumulating anaerobic interval workouts to just four or five weeks out of the year, at the most. Pre-pubescent children should do no anaerobic interval training. Arthur Lydiard was a critic of coaches who burn out young athletes mentally and physically with too much stressful lactic acid producing anaerobic interval work and over racing due to shortsighted goals. Take a long term approach.

At the end of the Race Phase is the **End of Season Recovery Phase**. This is a time to back way off to allow the athlete to mentally and physically recover from the season. This phase should last 1-2 weeks and consist of short and easy distance runs every other day. We do not advise doing the standard complete rest of 2 weeks or more. By doing a little running it allows the athlete to recover, but it also prevents them from needlessly losing the gains of the prior season/year. Fitness is lost much quicker than it is gained and it is not advisable to needlessly give back a significant amount of gains. In middle and distance running, you are always either getting better or getting worse. When you are doing nothing for 2 weeks or more, it doesn't require advanced scientific knowledge to know which direction you are heading. Not taking an extended layoff also reduces injury risk, because you are most at risk for injury when coming back from an extended lay-off. After the 2 week period, it is time to go back into the aerobic Base Phase and start the whole cycle over again.

SAMPLE PERIODIZED SCHEDULE FOR A TYPCIAL YOUTH RUNNER

This is the basic model Mick used to successfully develop youth athletes:

We set late July for our major target race, usually an outdoor track championship, and we will set up our training to peak at that competition. We have also set a "mini-peak" for a late November/Early December cross country (XC) championship. Occasionally, if we want to have a "mini-peak" during indoor track, we can set aside a small amount of training time to get ready for a specific race or two indoors. The primary goal for my kids during the winter is to not get hurt. Too many kids get injured indoors from doing too many races, too much anaerobic interval training in poor indoor facilities or poor weather conditions. It is better to safely continue to build an aerobic base, which results in superior long term development, rather than run anaerobic workouts and a ton of races.

August through November

- Primarily endurance base building, which consists of aerobic distance running, alternating slightly slower longer and slightly faster shorter runs, one or two tempo runs per week, and one or two long run per week (**covered in detail in Chapters 8 and 9**). One or two days also include working on basic speed (**see Chapter 14**). No anaerobic lactic acid training. Start with lower mileage and build up as possible within the guidelines outlined in **Chapter 8**.

- Incorporate hillier courses into training, 1 or 2 local tune-up XC races and Junior Olympic Cross Country Association and Regional races. Don't fall into the trap of over-racing. Races are fun and exciting for parents and coaches to WATCH, but kids get better by training, not running too many races. Resist this temptation. Remember aerobic endurance training is putting money in the bank, racing is taking money out of the bank. Spend it wisely.

December

- Taper and "mini-peak" for Junior Olympic Cross Country National Championships.

January through early June

- Continue endurance base building which primarily consists of aerobic distance running (alternating slightly slower longer and slightly faster shorter runs), one or two tempo runs per week, and one or two long runs per week (**see Chapters 8 and 9**). One or two days include working on basic speed (**see Chapter 14**). No anaerobic lactic acid training. Start out with lower mileage and build up as possible within the guidelines in **Chapter 8**. Consider a couple indoor races for fun and to keep the enthusiasm high. Resist the temptation to over-race.

Mid June to mid July

- Begin to slightly reduce mileage (10%) while beginning anaerobic phase (**see Chapter 10** for details on anaerobic interval training. Prepubescent kids should do no anaerobic interval training).
- Run Local and State Hershey track qualifying races leading up to the target race.

Mid July to Mid August

- Slightly reduce mileage (10%).
- Run Hershey's State Championship or Regional qualifying race for the Junior Olympics.
- Use one week taper to freshen for Junior Olympics or Hershey's North American track Championship.

Courtesy photo, Victah Sailer

Photo: Mick Grant's Lynx athletes sweeping the top places at the Boston Mayor's Cup XC Youth Race.
1st: Ashley Farnsworth, 2nd: Alison Travers, 3rd: Ashley Neville, 4th: Keely Maguire (far right). Maguire was one of 4 of Mick's athletes who went on to become Footlocker Finalists in XC. She also became a multiple New England Collegiate Champion in track at UNH, running a 4:45 mile, 9:29 3000, 16:27 5000 and 34:50 10000. Farnsworth was typical of Mick's athletes, showing great range in XC and track by running a 30 200 and 68 400 at age 10 and a 2:24 800 and 5:25 1600 at age 12.

8. AEROBIC BASE BUILDING

Never forget that aerobic endurance is the foundation to success for all race distances from 800 meter on up. How much mileage should I run during the Base Phase to build aerobic endurance? This is the question everyone wants answered. What is the magic number? When answering this question, always remember the first two rules laid out in **Chapter 1**, Have Fun and Stay Healthy. For beginning runners, it is best to start from zero, and gradually work up. If a young runner with no experience comes to practice, one to five minutes is fine. Some kids are not initially capable of running for 5 minutes without stopping. Have them walk and jog for a total of 5 minutes until they can get to the point where they can run for 5 minutes continuously. Eventually, they will be able to run one mile or more. The important thing is to keep the athlete healthy, so training can be consistent and increased gradually over time. Do not rush things with beginning runners. Rushing things invites two beginning runner's injuries - shin splints and Runner's Knee. It is simple logic that, if the athlete enjoys running and stays healthy and if the training load gradually increases over time, the training load will eventually become very high and the athlete very fit. Over time, our athlete will do more miles per run on average, more days per week, and at a faster aerobic pace.

There are too many factors involved to give specific cookie cutter guidelines on how many miles each athlete should run. However, to give no approximate guidelines on this critical subject would be a cop out. Again, the overriding determining factor in determining how much mileage is appropriate for each athlete is *FUN FIRST* and the health of the athlete. The young athlete must be enjoying what they are doing and must be healthy. The factors to determine how much mileage include:

- How much running have they done in the past?
- Age?
- Gender?
- What is their injury history if any?
- How much does the athlete feel comfortable with?
- How is the athlete responding to current mileage?
- How has the athlete responded to different mileage levels in the past?

- How is the athlete's diet? Are they taking in sufficient calories and nutrients?
- What is the athlete's current commitment level to the sport?
- How much time does the athlete have to devote to the sport?

Weekly Mileage Guidelines
Actual mileage is based upon factoring in all of the bullets listed above.

The athlete must progress through each stage. Do not take short-cuts. For example, if the athlete begins running at age 16, it is a good idea to begin with 5 minutes a day and gradually increase to 10-15 miles per week (MPW) and then later build up to a higher level. Do not just jump in at 50 MPW. Even though physically mature kids can handle more miles than physically immature kids, we still need to be patient and build up slowly. We need to stay healthy. Building up too rapidly could cause problems such as muscle strains from excessive muscle soreness, shin splints, or Runner's Knee.

The table shown below is the theoretical ideal progression for a youth runner to improve their aerobic endurance year after year after year. Keep in mind, this only applies to the theoretical ideal runner. Who is the theoretical ideal runner? It is a runner who starts running at a young age, and who loves to run, and enjoys the whole process, and whose enthusiasm increases every year, and due to the gradual build-up, rarely gets injured, and most importantly, shows a positive adaptation to the increased stimulus, meaning they get better every year.

Mileage Progression of the Theoretical Ideal Runner

Age	Days per week	Males MPW	Females MPW
6	3-7	3-7	3-7
7	3-7	3-10	3-10
8	3-7	6-15	6-15
9	3-7	6-16	6-16
10	3-7	8-18	8-18
11	3-7	10-20	10-20
12	4-7	15-25	15-25
13	4-7	25-35	25-35
14	5-7	35-45	35-45
15	6-7	45-55	40-50
16	6-7	50-60	45-55
17	7	55-65	50-60
18	7	65-75	55-65
19	7	75-85	60-70
20	7	85-95	65-75
21	7	100	80

Every runner won't fall into this model, so as a parent or coach you have to adapt the training to your kid. Some kids start at a later age and you always have to start at zero and gradually build them up, all the while ensuring they are enjoying it, they are staying healthy, and they are improving. In the above chart, the ideal athlete is spending an entire year at each mileage level. An athlete who starts at an older age can pass through each mileage level in less than a year PROVIDED they are enjoying it, staying healthy, improving at each mileage level, and are enthusiastic to move on to the next level. Even then, they should always spend a minimum of 2 months at each mileage level and even more months at each of the higher levels on the chart. Furthermore, they should not exceed the MPW levels shown in the chart for their age except in the rarest of circumstances. For example, say a 15 year old boy begins running for the first time. He would start out at 5 minutes a day for a couple of weeks, then progress to about 10 MPW for about a month, then 15 MPW for 2 months, then 20 MPW for 2 months, then 25 MPW for 2 months, etc. and by the end of their first year, they could be near 40 MPW. Again, as coach, you can't blindly follow a plan, you need to have a plan, then observe and adjust as necessary as you execute the plan. In this example, you have to pay attention and ask are they staying healthy, are they enjoying it, are they improving, do they want to move to the next level, etc.? If the answer is not yes to all of those questions, you should not be increasing mileage.

Some kids may not mentally enjoy increasing mileage to the next level, and you have to factor this into the training plan, so that the athlete and coach are on the same page. Again, have fun and stay healthy.

One of the most remarkable aspects of Coach Mick's career is how rare it was for his kids to have any injury trouble. Coach John's own kids Joe and Josh started at age 6 & 7 and have been running for 7 years, and neither has had a single injury following the guidelines of this book, and their enthusiasm for the sport grows every year, and they get better every year. However, some kids no matter how careful and gradual you are with their build-up, will have injury trouble. We will cover injury prevention and injuries more thoroughly in later chapters, but if a runner has recurring injury trouble, you cannot advance them to the next mileage level, until they successfully complete the current level, injury free for an extended period of time. Again, have fun and stay healthy.

Although it is rare, some runners will not continue to improve as you increase mileage. If this is the case, you need to evaluate everything they are doing; the runner's health, lifestyle, etc. and you will often find something is out of order and needs to be addressed. Always pay attention and make adjustments as necessary. Never blindly follow a plan.

Now that we have covered how to get started and covered MPW targets, we need to get into the details of what each week should look like during the Base Phase. The ideal to improve endurance is to run 7 days a week; however, some kids won't initially have the enthusiasm to run every day. If that is the case, start them out at 3 days a week and gradually progress them towards running every day over the months or years, as long as they are enjoying it. Again, have fun and stay healthy. Note that running less than 3 days a week will not result in ideal forward progress in developing the aerobic metabolism.

We want to get the athlete accustomed to running relaxed miles in the aerobic zone (which will be explained later in this chapter). What we aim for, during the endurance base phase training, is gradual, steady improvement through consistent training, not peaks and valleys. Once our athletes have been training for several weeks, it is beneficial during the endurance base phase to begin to vary the training distances each day. As time goes by, we will change training so that for example, instead of doing 5 miles every day, we will mix up the distance to begin developing a **Long Run**. For example, instead of doing 5 and 5, we might do 7 and 3. It is still 10 miles, but we have included a **Long Run** and a shorter recovery day. Arthur Lydiard discovered that we improve faster if we alternate distances by alternating longer days at a slightly slower pace and shorter days at a slightly faster pace. We call these shorter runs "recovery days" but we are still making progress. We recommend a weekly Long Run that is, for example, 20-25% of the weekly total. The purpose of the longer run is to increase the capillary density, the size of the heart, and the efficiency of the individual cells to utilize oxygen.

- **The purpose of Long Runs is to run far, not fast, and this should be the case throughout their Youth ages. Athletes older than age 20, who have more than 15,000 lifetime aerobic miles under their belt, and who are specifically training for the marathon, will incorporate fast long runs into the Anaerobic Phase of their training, but that is obviously outside the scope of this book.**

Once or twice each week, we will run at a faster pace. This is a run that is slightly below the threshold between aerobic and anaerobic running, which is why it is often called a "Threshold Run" or "At Threshold" (AT) or **"Tempo Run."** Lydiard called these runs "3/4 Effort" runs. This run is faster, but well within the capability of the runner and should not be like a race. The runner should be "pleasantly tired" at the end of the run as Arthur Lydiard liked to say. The purpose of the threshold run is to increase the stroke volume or the amount of blood pumped by each beat and to push the threshold out further and further over time. **Chapter 9** discusses threshold training in detail. Incorporating Long Runs and Threshold Training into the Base Phase results in huge improvement in the athlete, compared to the athlete who neglects one or both of these. This is a critical point for coaches and athletes to understand and incorporate into their Base Phase training. An athlete of equal raw talent, who is running the same MPW, but is running the same distance every day at the same pace, will fall way behind the runner, who is varying distances and doing long runs and tempo runs.

We also like to work on basic speed 1-2 days each week during the Base Phase. That will be detailed in **Chapter 14.**

What is Aerobic Running, anyway?

You want to do all your endurance training, including all daily distance runs, long runs, and threshold runs, in what is called the aerobic range, so let's go over some definitions.

Aerobic – Aerobic means with oxygen, so aerobic running is done at an effort in which the oxygen demands of the body are being met, and therefore, running can be done for an extended period of time at that effort. The body uses a combination of glycogen and fats for energy, which are broken down in the presence of oxygen.

Anaerobic – Anaerobic means without oxygen. When the effort is increased, eventually the oxygen demands of the body can no longer be met at the same rate it is being used. Gradually, the athlete will be in "oxygen debt" and will produce the waste product lactic acid.

Anaerobic Threshold – The Threshold is the blurry dividing line between aerobic running and anaerobic running. The line is blurry, because when you are running "aerobically", you are mostly using the aerobic energy system, but the anaerobic energy system is also operating, but at a very low level. As effort increases, the anaerobic energy system's contribution increases, but is still a minor contributor. At the "Threshold", the contribution of the anaerobic energy system spikes up dramatically, and the athlete will suddenly notice the production and accumulation of lactic acid with the slight burning sensation and/or heaviness in the muscles. At this point, the aerobic energy system is still being used, but the contribution of that system is equaled by the use of the anaerobic energy system.

Threshold Training – Threshold training or "Tempo" training is actually performed in the high aerobic range, up to but just below the Anaerobic Threshold. This type of training is extremely valuable because the athlete is working the very efficient aerobic energy system at a very high level. Because you are still in the aerobic range, you can maintain the effort for an extended period of time. Of course, even below the theoretical Anaerobic Threshold, the anaerobic system is working and producing relatively small amounts of lactic acid. For this reason, an athlete cannot effectively do this type of training every day without breaking down.

This is a key to success in training for middle and distance running. We will do all our distance training runs at an "aerobic effort" i.e. in the **Aerobic Range**. This is the single most important Lydiard principle and most misunderstood Lydiard principle. In the Base Phase, which is the bulk of our training, we won't ever be jogging (unless warming-up or cooling-down or rehabbing an injury), and we won't be going anaerobic or racing during our distance runs in practice. We want to be in the middle ground aerobic range between jogging and anaerobic running at all times.

Jogging is too slow for a competitive runner. While it is good for overall health and it burns fat, it does nothing for a competitive runner, because it takes way too long to see any improvement, because it doesn't stimulate the cardiovascular system enough. For 60 years, many people have misunderstood Lydiard and thought he was advocating jogging for training, as opposed to aerobic running including tempo runs, which he called "3/4 effort" runs. Expect to hear people to make the same mistake for decades to come, and you will tire of correcting them and arguing with them.

Anaerobic running and racing on distance runs is not good during the Base Phase, because you go into oxygen debt, and if you do more than two anaerobic runs in a row, your body starts breaking down.

The aerobic range is the ideal during Base Phase training, because you make continual progress, day after day. You can do it over the long term and see gradual improvement. You will be shocked how much you can improve, once you master running aerobically every day. There is no danger of burnout from distance training in the aerobic range. This is where we will do all our distance training. Keep in mind; everyone is at different levels, so a pace that is aerobic for some may be jogging for others and anaerobic for others. So you all need to discover your own aerobic rage. As you improve each week you will discover that your aerobic pace will be faster; so what was once an anaerobic pace will become aerobic for you later on, as you keep pushing your threshold out further. What was once aerobic, will become jogging pace for you after a few months. Gradually, you will be going faster for the same distance, with no extra effort.

So how do you know you are correctly in the aerobic range? It takes experience to learn it, but here are some clues to guide you. You should feel pleasantly tired at the end of the run. If you don't feel tired at all, you probably went too slow (i.e. jogging). If you feel wiped out and badly winded at the end of a run, you probably went too fast and crossed over into the anaerobic range. You will feel the heaviness and burning sensation of lactic acid creeping into your muscles when you cross the threshold. If you had to run the second half of the run slower than the first half, you went too fast and went anaerobic and had to slow down. You should always feel that you could have gone further and faster after the run. If not, you probably went anaerobic. In the aerobic range you should be able to hold a conversation. If you can gab easily, you are probably going too slow (i.e. jogging). If you cannot converse at all, you are probably going too fast and going anaerobic. For those of you familiar with heart rates or have heart monitors, the aerobic range for most people is a heart rate (HR) of 120 to 170 beats per minute. If your HR goes below 120, you are going too slow (i.e. just jogging). If it goes above 170 or if it spikes up during a distance run, you are probably going too fast and have gone anaerobic. It is often said that there is no secret in distance running, and that is pretty much true. The closest thing to "the secret" is the ability to learn to always run aerobically in the Base Phase. Those that master this and put in the miles day in and day out at a strong aerobic effort, are the ones who shock their fellow runners who will say, "How did they get so good?!!" Daily running at a strong aerobic effort is the secret, as it keeps pushing the aerobic/anaerobic threshold out further and further with each passing week. There is a close correlation between your race performance capability and where your aerobic/anaerobic threshold is.

There is also an important correlation between race performance capability and **Total Lifetime Accumulated Aerobic Miles** (provided there are no long sabbaticals from training). Those who have lots of money in the bank, i.e. lifetime accumulated aerobic miles, improve dramatically over the years. You don't see diminishing returns from aerobic mileage, until lifetime accumulated miles exceed 15,000 to 20,000 miles or more. Some people with 30,000 miles under their belt continue to see improvement. This is why it is an advantage to start young, and also why some of the East Africans, who started running to and from school from age 5 onward, often turn in such spectacular times in their late teens. It is because they have been running for almost 15 years already and have very high lifetime accumulated miles before age 20. Contrast them to the typical sedentary American lifestyle, where most kids don't start training until age 14, and who runs lots and lots of races and anaerobic workouts (and may be mentally burned out from all those races and workouts!), yet they have a relatively puny volume of lifetime accumulated aerobic miles, and it is easy to see the huge gulf between them and their East African counterparts.

So we have established that all your distance runs will be within the aerobic range. Within that range, we will vary pace slightly. Another one of Lydiard's important principles is to vary the distances each day. He found you improve much faster by running longer some days at a slightly slower, but still aerobic pace, and some days at a shorter distance, but at a slightly faster, but still aerobic pace. So some days you will be running at an easy aerobic pace, some days at a medium aerobic pace, and other days at a hard aerobic pace or tempo run. For short, we often just call them "easy", "medium", and "hard", but you need to remember you must always be in the aerobic range. So now I will explain the subtleties of easy vs. medium vs. hard. Easy will still be aerobic (i.e. faster than jogging) but at the low end of the aerobic range. Heart rate should be between 120 and 140. Conversing should be fairly easy. The weekly long run will be done at an easy aerobic pace and usually the day after the long run, and the day after tempo runs should be in the easy aerobic range.

Medium is a medium aerobic effort. Heart rate should be between 140 and 160, and you should be able to converse but not too easily. Some days should be in this range.

Hard is the tempo run (threshold run just below the aerobic/anaerobic threshold). You are still aerobic but at the high end, bumping up against the aerobic/anaerobic threshold, but below race pace. Don't sprint at the end. Heart rate should be 160 to 170 and not spike up as the run goes onward, but may drift up gradually. Conversation should be difficult and only intermittent, but not impossible. If you slow down on the second half, you probably went too hard early. So in a typical ideal week, you might have 1 or 2 high aerobic tempo runs, 3-4 low aerobic runs, including the Long Run and 1-3 medium aerobic runs. The exact breakdown will vary for each athlete, based on how they feel, and the coach's observation, and how they are responding to the training. Again, don't blindly follow a plan; have a plan, but observe and make adjustments as necessary.

Please note that the above HR guidelines only work for about 90% of runners. The other 10% will be **outliers** high or low, and also note that there is no correlation between talent and being in the normal range or being an outlier. Therefore, you don't want to be totally reliant on HR; you want to use a combination of HR, how the athlete feels, and the coach's observations as to how the athlete looks. Of these, how the athlete feels is the most important, especially once they become experienced enough to know when they are jogging, when they are in the aerobic range, and when they have crossed over into the anaerobic range. Over time, outliers and their coaches will learn what their individual HR ranges are for the various training speeds, i.e. what is normal for them.

Doubles

A commonly asked question is what about running twice a day? As the athlete continues to progress in the sport to higher levels and consequently higher weekly training mileage, at some point they need to consider doing "doubles" i.e. running twice a day. At the world class level, nearly 100% of all middle and distance runners the past 60 years, incorporated doubles to some extent into their training program. Depending on how far you want to go in the sport, and how committed you want to be, you eventually need to go to doubles.

Why do doubles?
- It is an easier way to increase mileage.
- It increases the number of runs per week, which increases overall cardiovascular stimulus.
- Any increase in the number of runs per week is often followed by improvement in fitness levels.
- Your average weekly training pace will be faster when doing doubles.
- You can't reach your ultimate potential in the sport without eventually doing doubles.

At what point in your career do you go to doubles? This is a controversial subject, and there is no one answer, and it depends on numerous factors. Here are some of our thoughts on the subject:
- No prepubescent youth runner should ever be doing doubles.
- No beginners should ever be doing doubles.
- No one should be doing doubles, until they have already been doing singles for at least a couple of years.
- No one doing 40 MPW or less should do doubles. Therefore, even someone following
   Our theoretical ideal mileage progression chart should not start doing doubles, until at least age 15.
- If you have severely restricted time windows for whatever reason, you may find doing doubles works for you.
- If the high school team or club you are running for is doing insufficient aerobic mileage for your long term development, you should consider doing doubles. Always get your coach's permission.

- Doing doubles is a significantly higher level of commitment, so be sure you are mentally and physically ready to go to that level, and that you will enjoy it.
- Coaches and parents should not push kids into doubles, until the kid is mentally and physically ready. Remember **FUN FIRST**.
- Once you get to 70 MPW or more, you should seriously consider adding doubles.
- Once you get to 100 MPW or more, you definitely should be doing doubles.
- When beginning doubles, always start with just one day for a few weeks and see how you respond to it. Most people experience tiredness initially, but the body will quickly adapt, and the tiredness will go away. As always, pay attention and never follow rigid plans.
- If you note a positive adaptation to the one day, then consider adding a second day, etc.
- Ensure at least 4 hours and 1 meal between doubles.
- Don't do doubles 7 days; the max is 6, because you need to continue to do Long Runs for as long as you are a competitive runner, so you need one day dedicated to long runs most of the year.

PRACTICE FOR NEW KIDS MADE EASIER

The easiest way to begin a youth program for brand new kids, one which will grow and thrive, is to run no more than five minutes at a time on your first day of practice (maybe the kids can run 5 minutes both at the beginning and at the end of practice). Mick likes to begin and end each practice with easy stretching, crunches, and push-ups. He also has them do 6 x 70 meter strides. Group the kids by current fitness level. Every month should include slightly more easy distance running (5 minutes, 6 minutes, 7 minutes, etc). Also, include a 3-5 minute easy cool-down run at the end of practice, if any fast running was done. We want to stress that if a new kid can only run for one minute, that is fine. Each week, the kids can run a little bit more.

- **Any starting point for new kids, for both distance and pace, is fine.**
- **Find out what the kids CAN DO and do that!**

The point is to develop a regular routine which is fun and includes a little bit of work. Mick would have them do 5-10 minutes of form drills each practice (See **Chapter 17**). Have some variety and make each practice slightly different within your regular routine. Have fun!

SAMPLE CHARTS SHOWING MILEAGE PROGRESSION FOR BEGINNERS

(10 year old new runner, no experience)

Month 1	3 days	1 mile per day	3 miles per week
Month 2	3 days	1.5 miles per day	4.5 miles
Month 3	3 days	2 miles per day	6 miles
Month 5	3 days	2 miles, 3 miles, 2 miles	7 miles
Month 7	3 days	3 miles, 4 miles, 3 miles	10 miles
Month 9	4 days	4-3-4-4	15 miles

(14 year old, no experience)

Week 1	3 days	1 mile per day	3 miles per week
Week 2	3 days	1.5 miles per day	4.5 miles
Week 3	3 days	2 miles per day	6 miles
Week 4	3 days	2 miles, 3 miles, 2 miles	7 miles
Month 2	3 days	3 miles, 4 miles, 3 miles	10 miles
Month 3	3 days	4 miles, 4 miles, 4 miles	12 miles
Month 5	4 days	4 miles, 5 miles, 4 miles, 5 miles	18 miles
Month 7	5 days	5 miles per day	25 miles
Month 9	6 days	6-4-5-5-6-4	30 miles

These are extremely simplified training charts. The point is to gradually run more miles.

- **The beginning point for a new runner should assume they have zero training background.**
- **Build on that.**

Young athletes with more experience could possibly be training at a somewhat higher level than this, but it is fine for a new kid to just run for one to five minutes, if that is all they can do.

Photo below: Mick's club kids putting in the aerobic miles on the trails of Winnekenni Park in Haverhill, MA. Left to right: Ashley Farnsworth, Keara Thomas, Alison Travers, Danny Wang and Pat Condon. Wang ran 1:55, 4:18 and 9:43 in high school and was a multiple NCAA All American in track and multiple NCAA XC qualifier in college at UMass-Lowell. The accomplishments of Farnsworth, Thomas, and Travers are listed in other photos in the book. **Courtesy photo/Lynx Elite Athletics**

Courtesy photo, Mick Grant

9. AEROBIC THRESHOLD TRAINING

Aerobic Threshold runs are a critical component of aerobic endurance base phase training. As stated previously, these runs go by various names, such as threshold runs, tempo runs, AT runs, Progressive Runs, Progressions, "3/4 effort" runs, etc. As explained in the definitions in **Chapter 8**, when you are in the aerobic range, oxygen supply meets oxygen demand, and the waste products produced are harmless carbon dioxide and water; but when you cross the threshold into the anaerobic range, oxygen supply is no longer meeting oxygen demand, so the waste product produced is lactic acid, and when it accumulates in the blood, it produces the burning sensation and heaviness in the muscles. We want to avoid that on tempo runs, and stay in the high end of the aerobic range. The purpose is to push the aerobic/anaerobic threshold out further and further as time passes. We do a tempo run once or twice per week close to the threshold pace, so aerobic improvement is accelerated. It is good to get the kids accustomed to a faster pace, so they can more easily move up to the next level. In addition to asking the athlete how they feel and observing how they look, we always check heart rate (HR) after tempo runs and sometimes during the workout, just to be sure we have the correct effort. We use tempo runs as a way to mix up the pace in training. We use a broader definition than many coaches. Depending on what we are training for, our tempo runs might be anywhere from 800 meters to 5 miles or more, and may be continuous, or broken up into segments, with a recovery jog interval in between each repetition. They can be steady state where you run about the same pace the whole way, or you run **negative splits,** meaning run each section faster than the previous section. This is called a **Progressive Tempo Run** or a "**Progression**". Older elite athletes may do 3 to 10 mile tempo runs, and marathoners may do 12-16 mile tempo runs during the base phase.

For our younger kids, a tempo run might be 800 meters at cross country race pace (or slower), after which we measure HR and adjust the pace as necessary for the next tempo run. Everything depends on the individual athlete. Tempo runs for young athletes should not be too demanding. We can even do one mile at a pace we have determined is appropriate for the athlete. We check heart rate regularly and are looking for the pace where heart rate "spikes up", which indicates that the athlete has gone anaerobic, which we want to avoid. It is important for young athletes to finish practice feeling that they have accomplished something positive. Small steps forward are very important. Tempo runs should be aerobic, not anaerobic. Many coaches do workouts that appear similar to ours on paper, but they are doing them in the anaerobic range, which means it is a completely different workout than we are doing. It is critically important that you learn this distinction and can recognize it in practice.

An example of a broken up tempo run for a pretty good 14 year old might be 5 x 800 meters with one minute rest interval. There are two reasons for the rest: 1. Check heart rate and 2. The interval pace can be faster than for a continuous one to three mile tempo run, so they get used to the faster pace. The times for the intervals could be 3:30, 3:20, 3:10, 3:00, 2:50 or they all could be at 3:10. The actual times don't matter as much as the effort being correctly in the high aerobic range, since the goal is gradual improvement. Again, it is critically important that the athlete and coach understand that doing the longer repeats in the high aerobic range is a completely different workout, than doing the same thing at a higher effort that turns it into an anaerobic interval workout. Those workouts should be limited to the anaerobic phase as explained in **Chapter 10**.

The athlete can start anywhere with tempo runs and gradually bring the times down over the weeks while maintaining the same effort. We want to keep the HR under control. We like our kids to be at least above 140 and usually below 165 HR range and definitely below 170. Times for future tempo runs are adjusted based on HR, and performance in previous tempo runs, and weather conditions, if applicable.

We can do any variation of this workout, including 3 x mile, 1 x 800, 1 x mile, or 1 x 800. We always want to run even or negative splits in tempo workouts. We don't want to run **positive splits,** where the athlete is slowing down during the workout. Slowing down means the athlete probably went too hard early and went anaerobic and was forced to slow down. If you notice an athlete slowing down during a tempo, stop the workout and adjust as necessary for the next time they do a tempo run. Negative splits means:

- The first part of the run or interval is the slowest.
- The last part of the run or interval is the fastest.

For example, Mick's athletes will run maybe 2 or 3 x 800m once they have advanced to the stage of beginning tempo running. Later as they progress, they do 4 mile tempo runs, on trails, at a medium to medium-high aerobic pace, determined by heart rate. Mick also uses a 2500 meter trail course, marked every 400m that is used as a high aerobic tempo run, and for learning 5k race pace. Over time, workouts will get faster, but HR will stay at 165 or lower for his athletes. Other examples include 3 mile tempos or alternately doing a 3 mile progression tempo, where each mile is run a few seconds faster than the previous mile. John has used for his sons 1 x 800 or 1 x 1.5 mile or 1 x 2 mile or 1 x 3 mile or 3 x mile tempo runs with an 800 jog recovery between the repeat miles. We have found improvement is accelerated when you vary the type of tempo, rather than using the same one all the time. Also, they get used to varying paces which results in further improvement. Needless to say, there are endless numbers of tempo runs you can come up with, but the single unifying rule for all tempo runs is that they remain in the high aerobic range.

During the aerobic base phase period, you should be doing at least one tempo run a week and often you can do two a week, provided they are done in the aerobic range, you have at least 2 easier aerobic days between them, and the athlete is responding positively to them, i.e. their times are coming down over time, even though they are using the same effort and are in the same HR range. Again, don't blindly follow a plan; observe and adjust as necessary.

Although out of the scope of this book, some older experienced elite athletes use unplanned tempo runs with great success. On the days during their base phase, when they happen to feel good early in a run, they will launch into a spontaneous tempo or progression run a couple times a week. In the era before the terms such as tempo run came into use, they were simply called "hammering" or "running to the barn". Needless to say this method would not work for typical inexperienced youth runners, because they would run them too often, or not often enough, or too slow or too fast, or on back to back days, or some bad combination of too slow and too fast.

In conclusion, we use tempo runs at a variety of paces to push high aerobic work. It is a good way to break up the daily grind of mileage, adds variety to the training regimen, and gets the kids used to running at a faster pace. Over time, we can make remarkable progress, by pushing the anaerobic threshold out further and further. We do not want to be anaerobic. Guard against kids competing with each other in these workouts and turning them into anaerobic runs. Going anaerobic will cause overall quality to deteriorate, will require more recovery, and is taking money out of the bank. There is a time for anaerobic training but not during the base phase. As stated previously, note that there is no clear exact line where running goes from purely 100%

aerobic to purely 100% anaerobic. Even easy aerobic running is slightly anaerobic and even when you are running very hard anaerobically, you are also still stimulating the aerobic metabolism. The line (or threshold) is a blurry line where, if you increase the pace beyond that, you will see a spike up in lactic acid production, a rapid rise in HR, and will feel the lactic acid burning and/or "heaviness" in your muscles.

The coach and athlete should use 4 methods to determine if the athlete ran in the appropriate high aerobic range:

1) How the athlete felt - Were they pleasantly tired, and feeling good, or was it too hard and were they wiped out or seemed like they were working too hard? Did they feel the burn of the lactic acid and the heaviness of the lactic acid in the muscles?

2) How the coach felt the athlete looked - Were they in control and still able to talk a little, or were they breathing excessively, or was their form falling apart, or did they appear to be straining too hard?

3) The heart rate - Should be between 145 and 165 and definitely lower than 170.

4) What pace they ran - Was it in line with what you expected based on their current fitness and previous tempo runs and the weather conditions? If they ran the second half slower, that is an indication they went too fast.

Tempo Run Rules

- ✓ You want to be in the high end of the aerobic range. Don't cross the threshold into the anaerobic range, where lactic acid rapidly builds up, and each minute of running gets harder and harder, as it does in a race, or when you do anaerobic interval workouts. You don't want that to happen on tempo runs.
- ✓ Heart rate should always be under 174 (we try for 165 to be safe). Check your heart rate at the end by putting your fingers on your neck and counting the beats for 10 seconds, then multiply by 6 to get the beats per minute.
- ✓ Effort should be 70-80% of an all out race effort, never harder than that, when in doubt slow down.
- ✓ Focus on the effort and how you feel, not going for a particular time. Any time goals are just a guide. Also the weather conditions are another factor affecting time.
- ✓ If you start to feel uncomfortable, or you start feeling the burn or heaviness of the lactic acid, or if it is impossible for you talk

a little bit during the tempo run, you are probably going too fast, and have crossed the threshold and need to slow down.

✓ Don't sprint at the end.

✓ Run even splits (each mile in the same time) or slightly negative splits. Negative splits means running the second half faster than the first half. This is called a Progressive Tempo Run.

✓ If you end up running the second half slower than the first half, you went out too fast and went anaerobic, which defeats the purpose of the tempo run.

✓ You should feel what Arthur Lydiard termed "pleasantly tired" at the end, not wiped out.

✓ You should always feel at the end that you could have gone faster if you had to, or would have been able to maintain the same pace for longer if you had to.

✓ When in doubt, slow down.

✓ Don't cross over the aerobic/anaerobic threshold just to meet some goal time.

✓ Keep your ego at bay. You need the confidence to run these correctly. Do not worry about running a great time, running faster than some teammate or some other runner did, and do not try to impress the coach, your teammates, or yourself.

✓ Be patient; you will be doing many months of tempo runs; don't try to set the world on fire on them. Relax, be confident and patient, and enjoy the process. Don't rush things.

✓ If you feel really good, don't increase pace early in the run, be patient and wait until the second half of the run to slightly increase the pace.

✓ Remember that if you run these correctly, i.e. just below the aerobic/anaerobic threshold, you will get better and better each week, and you will be amazed by how much you will improve, when you combine this with running every day, and also doing the Long Run. Also, if you consistently cross the threshold and go anaerobic on these runs, either deliberately or without realizing it, it is like running a race every week. You will rapidly peak at a much lower level, will stagnate, and could become mentally and physically burned out, before the end of the racing season. Again, when in doubt, slow down. If you are going to make a mistake on these tempo runs, it is better to run too slow than too fast.

✓ Don't worry or obsess about the times on tempo runs. What you perceive as a bad tempo may still be good, because you got the effort in. Your body will adapt and improve, even if you think you should have been able to run a faster time.

Photo: Alanna Poretta, running for her high school in the mile versus Abbey D'Agostino. Poretta ran a 2:24 800 in Junior High, was a Hershey Regional 800 Champion, Hershey Nationals 800 Finalist, Junior Olympics 800 New England Champion, sub 5 minute miler, and became a Massachusetts State XC Champion.

Courtesy photo, Lynx Elite Athletics/Jon Moulton

10. ANAEROBIC PHASE

- **We don't recommend EVER trying to ramp up miles while in the anaerobic workout phase.**

As we have stated repeatedly throughout this book, we are more interested in the long term development of athletes, than short term results. Therefore, our athletes work on endurance (**see Chapters 8 and 9**) and basic speed (**see Chapter 14**) most of the year, not demanding, lactic acid accumulating, anaerobic workouts. Young kids, age 13 and under, are better off doing no anaerobic interval training at all. Anaerobic training is very demanding, and should be gradually introduced only after the kids have built a good aerobic foundation. As we just mentioned, our young prepubescent kids do no anaerobic interval training.

Our older, more conditioned, athletes cannot race at their best, however, without doing two to four weeks of anaerobic interval training leading up to our target race. Arthur Lydiard called anaerobic interval training the "Icing on the Cake." These types of workouts produce quick but temporary results, and are most effective when we have first taken the time to build an adequate endurance base. Unfortunately, there are many coaches who see these quick results and don't realize they are temporary and try to make anaerobic interval training the core of their program for the entire school year. The problem is, although they may enjoy good early season results, improvement ceases, because there is not a well developed endurance base. Additionally, because of the temporary nature anaerobic workouts produce, the athlete may show little improvement from year to year, other than that due to normal physical maturation that comes with age.

Warning!!!! Avoid Mental Burnout !!!

Burnout – Burnout is a condition to be avoided at all costs, and every year it ruins the joy and/or careers of thousands of youth middle and long distance runners. Burnout is also called various layman's terms commonly used in the sport such as "breaking down", "going past your peak", "peaking too soon", "falling apart", or being "fried" or "toast". Burn out is caused by too many all out races and/or too much anaerobic interval training. It is not caused by running too much aerobic mileage, even at very high levels. Many people confuse this critical distinction, and when discussing burnout erroneously, mix them all together and confuse themselves and others. Even moderate frequency of racing and moderate frequency anaerobic interval training, can result in burnout, if it is carried on for too many weeks.

Anaerobic workouts put significant stress on the Central Nervous System[1], so if we keep this stress on the young athlete for too many weeks, negative side effects often referred to as "overtraining" may appear, including illness, poor race performance, prolonged elevated resting heart rate, irritability, interrupted sleep patterns, loss of appetite, loss of desire to train or race, and even mild depression. It also causes the athlete to peak way too soon in the season, well before the most important races, and also the peak is too low. It also heightens the risk of a running related injury. Unfortunately, the structure of the American High School XC/Track Race season almost guarantees a high percentage of athletes will burnout during the school year. A typical program takes on the nearly impossible task of trying to peak 3 times in a school year for XC, indoor track, and outdoor track, and involves practically non-stop racing from early September to early June. Combine this heavy anaerobic race load with way too much anaerobic interval training and not enough aerobic base work, and you have the perfect recipe for disaster.

Indeed the result was a disaster for American high school distance running. For example, in the 1970s there were consistently more than 20 kids breaking 9 minutes in the 2 mile every year. Then in the 1980s and early '90s, the "Quality, Not Quantity" mantra pushed by some mainstream running magazines became prevalent and most coaches believed "quality" meant more and more killer anaerobic interval training (as opposed to more high aerobic threshold runs), and the "quantity" to be eliminated was aerobic base miles. The result was an unmitigated disaster for the sport as a whole, with the number of kids breaking 9 minutes plummeting to just a handful per year by the mid 1990s, when American distance running finally bottomed. Thanks to the internet, many coaches (though still a small percentage of all coaches) rediscovered Lydiard and the benefits of aerobic base training and found innovative ways to work around the crazy American High School race structure, and you are seeing similar results at the high end to the 1970s again. Still, the vast majority of

---

[1] Running With Lydiard, Lydiard & Gilmour, Hodder and Stoughton

Press, 1983, pg 13

coaches have not caught on to the correct way to train. Ironically, star youth athletes are at even higher risk. When such athletes are running really fast times at age 14 or so, the coaches wrongly assume they can handle much higher volume of races and anaerobic work, and pressure to "score points", and forget they are just kids, with still developing bodies, and they sometimes ruin great potential.

Therefore, as a coach or parent, you have to be always on guard against too many races and too much anaerobic interval training.

- **If we notice any "backsliding" in performance, we must immediately stop the anaerobic phase and/or race phase and allow for recovery and easy running. Yes, this is a bitter pill to swallow for both coach and athlete, with the only solace being, you will be a little wiser the next season.**
- **Remember these words of wisdom, "When you find yourself in a hole, stop digging."**

For Young athletes, we recommend spending 90% of the year working on endurance (**Chapters 8 and 9**) and basic speed (**Chapter 14**) and only 10% of the year on lactic acid producing anaerobic workouts, as outlined in this chapter. This is the phase where the biggest and costliest mistakes are often made. You may be asking, "Why do any such workouts?" In order to sharpen up, or "peak," we must do some anaerobic work. Middle and distance races are run at speeds that will produce lots of lactic acid. Lactic acid is the burning, heavy feeling in tiring muscles from intense exercise. It is caused once we go into "Oxygen Debt." If we run a race without any prior anaerobic training, our body will be unprepared for the sudden lactic acid accumulation, and we won't race up to our potential. Therefore, we must complete some anaerobic training prior to the target race.

In conclusion, we focus on endurance training most of the year, for the long term gains of developing the aerobic/anaerobic threshold, so we can run further and faster aerobically. Then, prior to our target race, we will complete some anaerobic "peaking" workouts, for the temporary benefit of producing the buffering agents to cope with lactic acid, and performance is maximized. We believe that, for most young athletes, peak performance will be reached within one month of the commencement of the anaerobic phase.

The next question is, how long can a young athlete hold a peak? This depends on the age of the athlete, the endurance base, the number of and distance of races, and other factors. We believe young athletes can hold a peak for no more than 2 to 4 weeks.

Categorizing Aerobic Training

Jogging: Normally not part of our training, unless part of recovering from injury or overtraining, because the pace is too slow to be beneficial for aerobic development. HR below 120.

Aerobic Endurance: Regular, daily distance running at a steady (conversational) pace. HR 120-160.

Tempo Runs: High aerobic effort at faster than normal pace, but just under the anaerobic threshold. These can consist of continuous running for a set distance or aerobic intervals. HR 160-170 (we prefer to keep under 165).

Fartlek: "Speed Play" can be aerobic or anaerobic. Can be structured or unstructured. When done at a relatively lower intensity level, it is a form of high aerobic training. This is not normally recommended for Youth athletes, because they don't have the experience to properly execute the run to meet the desired training effect.

Categorizing Anaerobic Training

Basic Speed: Short intervals of 200 meter or less at faster than 800 meter race pace - the shorter the faster. Note that even though these are technically anaerobic, they are short enough distance, and the recovery between each rep is long enough, such that no lactic acid accumulates, and hence they are call alactic basic speed work, and we use them throughout the aerobic base phase (i.e. most of the year) to improve basic speed (**see chapter 14**). Short hill repeats with long recoveries, also fall into this category.

Anaerobic Intervals: There are three general types, and note that subtle changes in the workout can change them to a different category:

1) "Long Intervals": Consists of running repetitions close to race pace, which are commonly called "long intervals", with relatively longer recovery jog intervals between each repetition. These are also called "VO2 Max" intervals. In general, these should be done early in the anaerobic phase. They are not to be confused with segmented or broken up tempo runs, used in the base phase, that look similar, but are at a lower effort, so a different type of workout.

2) "Short Intervals": Consists of shorter repetitions at race pace or slightly faster, which are commonly called "short intervals". In general, these should be done in the middle and later stages of the anaerobic phase.

3) "Peaking Workouts": Consists of repetitions with a very short recovery interval, which drive the runner deep into oxygen debt to stimulate a peak. These must be restricted to the final two weeks prior

to the target race, and obviously should be used sparingly. They can be long and hard, such as repeat 400's, with only a 100 meter recovery jog or "Aussie Quarters", where the recovery interval is not much slower than race pace. Such workouts should be done at about 10 days before the target race. Within 10 days of the target race, the athlete may not recover in time for the race. Peaking workouts can also be short and hard such as "Lydiard Sharpeners", where you sprint for 50 meters, then float for 50 meters for a few laps on the track, or 3 x 400, or 2 x 800 etc., much faster than race pace, with only a 1 minute recovery. These can be done within the last 10 days before the target race, as long as there is still 3 easy recovery days between the workout and the target race. Alternately, consider just doing pacing workouts in the last 10 days, if your athlete already appears sharp and is already at or ahead of where you expected them to be, before the season started. This is where caution is warranted; don't get greedy and ruin a good thing. So instead of doing a short hard peaking workout 4 days before the target race for an 800 runner, just do for example 4 x 200 at 800 race pace. Mick had great success just using pacing workouts with his athletes in the last 10 days.

Anaerobic "Long intervals" ("VO2 Max Intervals) are highly effective and recommended early in the anaerobic phase. As described earlier in **Chapter 9,** no running is purely aerobic or anaerobic. When doing tempo runs such a 3M at steady pace or 3 x 1 mile repeats, as long as you keep your HR below 170, the workout is mostly aerobic, even though the anaerobic system is working at a low level. When you run for example the 3 x 1 mile repeats faster and at such an effort that you cross the threshold into anaerobic territory, now the anaerobic system is the major contributor, but the aerobic system is still working and working at a high level. Because of this, doing "long intervals" in the anaerobic range i.e. VO2 Max Intervals causes you to not only train the anaerobic system, but also simultaneously work the aerobic system at a high level so there is a dual effect. This makes anaerobic "long intervals" (VO2 Max Intervals) one of, if not the most effective tools during the anaerobic phase. Some coaches may not know the science behind it, but they certainly know how effective the results can be. However, because of the anaerobic nature of the workout, the athlete will break down if this training is carried on for too many weeks. It is very important that the coach understands the difference between aerobic tempo run long intervals, and anaerobic long intervals

(VO2 Max Intervals), and to use each of them properly, and during the correct phase of training.

Hills: Usually repeats up a hill and jogging back down. These were favored by Lydiard as a transition from the endurance base phase to the heavy anaerobic phase on the track. They can be either anaerobic, if the hills are long and/or recovery is short or alactic basic speed work, if the hill is short and the recovery is long. When done anerobically later in the anaerobic phase, this training can be highly effective preparation for hilly cross country races.

Fartlek: Done at a higher intensity level, can be an anaerobic workout. (See fartlek description above.)

How do we go about anaerobic training?   There are so many ways to do it.
Let's start with a list of Do's and Don'ts:

- **Don't** ever ramp up miles while doing anaerobic workouts. We cannot increase mileage while simultaneously doing anaerobic training. This puts too much stress on the body and is a recipe for disaster.   In most cases, you want to be decreasing mileage during this phase. You want to keep doing mileage and keep doing weekly long run to maintain your endurance base, but you should reduce both total mileage and the length of the long run during this phase, otherwise what is called the "**intensity density**" will be too high, and the runner will break down or get injured.
- **Don't** do anaerobic workouts for more than four or five weeks.
- **Don't** do anaerobic workouts on consecutive days. We need at least one or two recovery days between each anaerobic workout.
- **Don't** do more than 2 anaerobic workouts per week.
- **Don't** push too hard. As Lydiard says, "Train, don't strain."
- **Don't** stick to rigid time goals or number of intervals. Stop when performance slips.
- **Don't** do anaerobic workouts without first developing a solid aerobic endurance base.
- **Don't** have prepubescent kids do any anaerobic training, as they are not mature enough to handle it. Instead, have them focus on building endurance and improving basic speed.

- **Don't** do the same interval workout every week, because the athletes will adapt to that specific workout, and you don't want athletes getting good at a specific interval workout; you want them to improve their anaerobic capacity so they can race well.

- **Do** decrease your mileage and the length of the long run once starting the anaerobic phase.
- **Do** continue endurance runs to maintain your endurance base.
- **Do** take at least one or two easy recovery days between each hard workout.
- **Do** about two to four weeks of the anaerobic phase prior to the target race. That is plenty for a youth runner. The length of the phase will depend on the age of the athlete, their endurance base, and most importantly, how they are responding to the training. We feel that for most young athletes, even those with a good aerobic base, once anaerobic workouts are begun, the peak performance will be reached within a month. After that, performance will frequently begin to slip. Therefore, it is important to properly time the beginning of the anaerobic phase. Older athletes with a large endurance base and high lifetime accumulated aerobic miles can handle a longer combined anaerobic/race phase of 6-10 weeks, but that is outside the scope of this book. However, even for them going longer than 8 weeks, could result in the wheels coming off too soon. Always err on the side of caution in the anaerobic phase, because this is where the most costly mistakes are made.
- **Do** a total of repetitions that add up to approximately the goal race distance.
- **Do** jog a recovery between each interval that takes about as long as the interval. We want extra rest to ensure hitting the interval times and not wearing down the athlete.
- **Do** learn how to run negative splits in interval training. We always run each interval slightly faster than the previous one. This is excellent mental training.
- **Do** make the first workouts easier and gradually increase the intensity. Ensure that workouts are always well within the capability of the athlete. We need to be sure our athlete is responding positively to the training. Pay attention!
- **Do** start with long intervals (VO2 Max Intervals) earlier in the phase and progress to shorter, faster intervals later in the phase. As explained above, longer intervals (VO2 Max Intervals) are

highly effective early in the anaerobic phase because they stimulate both the anaerobic AND aerobic systems simultaneously. Coaches who use these may not know the science behind it but they certainly know the short term effectiveness of anaerobic long intervals.

- **Do** some anaerobic work at least once every 5 days once you start doing anaerobic work. This is one of the many double edges swords of anaerobic work. Once you start doing anaerobic work you must continue to do it (or have a race scheduled) at least every 5 days or it will lose its effectiveness. This is why it is critically important to not start the anaerobic phase too soon or carry it on for too long.

- **Do** a concentrated anaerobic phase for best results rather than a long drawn out phase. For example, it is far better to have 6 combined weeks of anaerobic workouts and races including 4-5 all out races, than to have a 12 week period where the anaerobic workouts and 4-5 races are spread out. The reasons are multiple. It is better to use the extra 6 weeks for aerobic base training, i.e. for long term improvement. If you don't provide anaerobic stimulus at least every 5 days, its effectiveness will be greatly reduced and if you do it at least every 5 days, 12 weeks is way too long to carry it out putting too much stress for too long on the runner's Central Nervous System and the runner will peak too soon or burnout or worse. Don't try to spread out the anaerobic/race phases, concentrated phases are much more effective.

- **Do** the final long and hard anaerobic peaking workout about 10 days prior to the target race. After this, recovery time is inadequate for full recovery before the target race. Any workout after this should be short and fast and/or not too hard, so they get some anaerobic stimulus, so they don't lose anything, but easy enough so they quickly recover in time for the target race. The last workout of any kind, should be 3-4 days before the target race. After that, only short easy runs.

- **Do** consider just doing pacing workouts in the last 10 days, if your athlete already appears sharp, and is already at or ahead of where you expected them to be, before the season started. This is where caution is warranted; don't get greedy and ruin a good thing. Instead of doing a short hard peaking workout 4 days before the target race, for an 800 runner, just do for example 4 x 200 at 800 race pace.

- **Do** cut mileage back in the last 7-14 days to taper. At this point you are trying to freshen and peak and mileage won't help you in the short term for the target race.
- **Do** monitor your athletes during the last 10 days. Some athletes get nervous and feel they need to train more, and we want to prevent this.

We don't need a track for intervals; we can do them in a park or on trails or on roads. As the sarcastic saying goes, a track is only to make it easy and convenient for the coach. We don't even have to know the exact distance. We just want to run fast enough to produce the lactic acid. It doesn't need to be exact or complicated. If the target race is a cross country race, we want to do many of these workouts on terrain that is close to what will be encountered. For example, if it is a very hilly course, we want to do some of these workouts on a hilly course.

Photo: Mia Swenson, who was coached by Mick Grant, breaking 5 minutes in the mile for the first time. Like most of Mick's runners, Mia had great range running a 2:15 800. She was also her high school's valedictorian. At Princeton she qualified for the NCAA XC Championships. Mia also has run a sub 3 hour marathon.
Courtesy photo, Alison Wade/New York Road Runners

11. SAMPLE ANAEROBIC WORKOUTS

Please note, there are an infinite number of anaerobic interval workouts one can devise, and as long as your follow the guidelines of **Chapter 10**, the details you pick are not important. You can make the workouts complicated or simple, and if you follow the basic guidelines above, they will be equally effective. Here are some simple examples of workouts, but do not attempt all of these workouts; there are way too many, pick and do just a few that you will feel will work best for your particular athlete:

800M

(300m and under is slightly faster than race pace, 400m and up is slightly slower than race pace)

"Long Intervals" favored early in the anaerobic phase

2 x 600 (300 jog) This means run a 600 meter close to race pace, then do a 300 meter recovery jog interval, then do another 600 at close to race pace.

3 x 400 (200 jog)

2 x 400 (200 jog)

400, 3 x 200 (200 jog)

Short Intervals favored later in the anaerobic phase

6 x 200 (200 jog)

3 x 300 (100 jog)

4 x 200 (200 jog)

8-10 x 100 (100 jog)

Peaking workouts favored in the last 2 weeks

4 x 200 (30 sec rest)

6 x 100 (15 sec rest)

Lydiard Sharpeners: 2 laps of sprint 50/float 50 (only use late in season)

400 much faster than race pace (1 min rest) then 2 x 200 much faster than race pace (30 second rest). Use only once per season, just before championship

1500M / Mile

(600m and under is slightly faster than race pace, 800m and up is slightly slower than race pace)

"Long Intervals" favored early in the anaerobic phase

3 x 800 (400 jog)

1200 (600 jog), 800 (400 jog), 400

2 x 800 (400 jog)

600, 400, 300, 200, 100 (200 jog)

800 (400 jog), 3 x 400 (200 jog)

<u>Short Intervals favored later in the anaerobic phase</u>

4-6 x 400 (200 jog)

3x 400 (200 jog)

8 x 200 (200 jog)

<u>Peaking workouts favored in the last 2 weeks</u>

6 x 400 (100 jog)   (don't use within 10 days of championship, won't recover in time)

Aussie Quarters 3 x 400 at race pace (200 fast recovery), 200 recovery done at only 7-12 seconds slower than race pace (don't use within 10 days of championship, won't recover in time)

Lydiard Sharpeners: 3-4 laps of sprint 50/float 50 (only use late in season)

3 x 400 much faster than race pace (1 min rest). Use only once per season, just before championship.

3000M / 2 Mile

(1200m and under is slightly faster than race pace, mile and up is slightly slower than race pace)

<u>"Long Intervals" favored early in the anaerobic phase</u>

3 x mile (800 jog)

2 x mile (800 jog)

mile (800 jog), 3 x 800 (400 jog)

4 x 800 (400 jog)

<u>Short Intervals favored later in the anaerobic phase</u>

8 x 400 (200 jog)

16 x 200 (200 jog)

<u>Peaking workouts favored in the last 2 weeks</u>

Aussie Quarters 6 x 400 at race pace (200 fast recovery), 200 recovery done at only 7-12 seconds slower than race pace (don't use within 10 days of championship, won't recover in time)

Lydiard Sharpeners: 5-6 laps of sprint 50/float 50 (only use late in season)

800 much faster than race pace (2 min rest), 2 x 400 much faster than race pace (1 min rest) Use only once per season, just before championship.

2K (Youth) XC

<u>"Long Intervals" favored early in the anaerobic phase</u>

mile (800 jog), 800 on grass or trails

2 x 1000 (800 jog) on grass or trails

<u>Short Intervals favored later in the anaerobic phase</u>

2-3 x 800 (400 jog) on grass or trails

1 x 1000 on grass or trails
Peaking workouts favored in the last 2 weeks
5-6 x 400 (200 jog) on grass or trails
2-5 x 60-100 meter steep hill (jog down), only do late in season, within 10 days prior to championship, if race is on hilly course.

4K (Youth) XC

"Long Intervals" favored early in the anaerobic phase
3 x mile (800 jog) on grass or trails
mile (800 jog), 3 x 800 (400 jog) on grass or trails
4 x 1000 (800 jog) on grass or trails
5 x 800 (400 jog) on grass or trails
Short Intervals favored later in the anaerobic phase
1 x 2000 on grass or trails
10 x 400 (200 jog) on grass or trails
Peaking workouts favored in the last 2 weeks
2 x 800 very fast (2 min rest) on track or trails
2-5 x 60-100 meter steep hill (jog down), only do late in season, within 10 days prior to championship, if race is on hilly course.

5K/6K XC

"Long Intervals" favored early in the anaerobic phase
3 x 2000 (1000 jog) on grass or trails
3 x mile (800 jog) on grass or trails
5 x 1000 (500 jog) on grass or trails
6 x 800 (400 jog) on grass or trails
Short Intervals favored later in the anaerobic phase
12 x 400 (200 jog) on grass or trails
1 x 1.5K on grass or trails
Peaking workouts favored in the last 2 weeks
2 x 800 very fast (2 min rest) on track or trails
4-8 x 60-100 meter steep hill (jog down), only do late in season, within 10 days prior to championship, if race is on hilly course.

8K/5M/10K XC

Note: No Youth runners (16 and under) should ever be running races longer than 5000 meters, except in the rarest of circumstances, where the runner is already at an elite level, and has at least 10000 miles of accumulated training miles in their lifetime. Otherwise, they should focus on getting faster at shorter distances, and building endurance, until they are older.

(Mile and under is slightly faster than race pace, over a mile is slower than race pace)

"Long Intervals" favored early in the anaerobic phase

4-6 x 2000 (1000 jog) on grass or trails

4-5 x mile (800 jog) on grass or trails

6-8 x 1000 (500 jog) on grass or trails

Short Intervals favored later in the anaerobic phase

8-10 x 800 (400 jog) on grass or trails

12 x 400 (200 jog) on grass or trails

Peaking workouts favored in the last 2 weeks

6-8 x 400 very fast (200 jog) on grass or trails

2 x 800 very fast (2 min rest) on track or trails

4-8 x 60-100 meter steep hill (jog down), only do late in season, within 10 days prior to championship, if race is on hilly course.

5000M

(Mile and under is slightly faster than race pace, over a mile is slower than race pace)

"Long Intervals" favored early in the anaerobic phase

3 x mile (800 jog)

mile (800 jog), 4 x 800 (400 jog)

5 x 1000 (600 jog)

6 x 800 (400 jog)

Short Intervals favored later in the anaerobic phase

12 x 400 (200 jog)

20 x 200 (200 jog)

Peaking workouts favored in the last 2 weeks

12 x 400 (100 jog), only use this workout late in season (don't use within 10 days of championship, won't recover in time)

Aussie Quarters 8 x 400 at race pace (200 fast recovery), 200 recovery done at only 7-12 seconds slower than race pace (don't use within 10 days of championship, won't recover in time)

Lydiard Sharpeners: 5-6 laps of sprint 50/float 50 (only use late in season)

10000M

Note: No Youth runners (16 and under) should ever be running races longer than 5000 meters, except in the rarest of circumstances, where the runner is already at an elite level, and has at least 10000 miles of accumulated training miles in their lifetime. Otherwise, they should focus on getting faster at shorter distances, and building endurance until they are older.

(Mile and under is slightly faster than race pace, over a mile is slower than race pace)

"Long Intervals" favored early in the anaerobic phase
5 x 2000 (800 jog)
6 x mile (800 jog)
3 x mile (400 jog)
Short Intervals favored later in the anaerobic phase
8-12 x 800 (400 jog)
12-20 x 400 (200 jog)
20 x 200 (200 jog)
Peaking workouts favored in the last 2 weeks
12 x 400 (100 jog), only use this workout late in season (don't use within 10 days of championship, won't recover in time)
Aussie Quarters 16 x 400 at race pace (200 fast recovery), 200 recovery done at only 7-12 seconds slower than race pace (don't use within 10 days of championship, won't recover in time)
Lydiard Sharpeners: 5-6 laps of sprint 50/float 50 (only use late in season)

Marathon

Note: No Youth runners (20 and under) should ever be running a marathon, but we are providing sample workouts for older runners who are reading the book and are interested in the marathon.
Early in anaerobic phase
3 x 4 mile (5 min jog) slower than marathon pace
4 x 3 mile (5 min jog) slightly slower than marathon pace
6 x 2 mile (5 min jog) at marathon pace
8 x 1 mile (3 min jog) faster than marathon pace
Later in anaerobic phase
24-28 miles at slower than marathon pace
12 miles at slightly faster than marathon pace
half marathon race
15 miles at marathon race pace
18-22 miles at slightly slower than marathon pace (leave at least 15 days before marathon)

Pacing for Interval Training

In general the pace of the repetitions during anaerobic interval training should be close to the specific goal race pace. That said, minor modifications to that general rule should be implemented. Early in the anaerobic interval phase, they should start out slightly slower than goal race pace, and during the middle of the phase, increase to exactly on race goal pace, and later in the phase, to slightly faster than race pace. Also, when doing longer intervals, the pace should be slightly slower, than when doing shorter intervals, which should be slightly faster, but always be working near the approximate goal race pace. When close to championship time, an effective tool is to do a short but very fast workout much faster than race pace that drives the athlete deep into oxygen debt to stimulate a peak. You obviously want to use these sparingly and only late in the season, and you must ensure full recovery can be attained prior to the target race, which means 3-4 days before the target race. Alternately, if you athlete is very sharp, it is wise just to do easy pacing intervals right at race pace in the last 10 days.

Regardless of these pace guidelines, the general rules for anaerobic interval training always override any pace or number of repetitions goals. Train, but do not strain. **The effort MUST be less than race effort at all times. It is critically important that both athlete and coach always recognize that a race effort should ALWAYS be significantly higher than a workout effort.** Don't make the frequent mistake of leaving your season's best performance in a workout and not in a race. This must be avoided at all cost. Tough athletes are a pleasure to coach, but they must be reigned in during workouts.

If performance drops off, stop the workout; they have had enough for the day. Factor in the environmental conditions (heat, humidity, cold, wind, rain, surface condition etc.); don't blindly try to meet times. Don't ever do killer workouts. If the pre-determined pace turns out be too hard for their current condition and/or weather conditions, slow the times down. Whenever in doubt during anaerobic interval training, slow things down or cut them short as necessary. Never lose sight of the big picture of the purpose of anaerobic interval training, which is simply to get the athlete into debt to stimulate the production of lactic acid buffering agents, so they can race at their best. There is no need to fret over the details or overly complicate things.

12. RECOVERY

Simply put, athletes CANNOT improve without recovery. This sounds contrary to everything distance runners stand for, but it is perfectly logical. For example, if a 12 year old can run 13 miles, should he run 13 miles per day, every day, in order to get good? It is logical to believe that a 12 year old running that much would break down and/or get injured pretty quickly.

By recovery, we don't mean taking days off completely from running, but by doing relatively easy running in the low aerobic range. The trick is to mix harder and easier days to allow for muscular recovery. When an athlete is subjected to a taxing run such as the weekly Long Run, during the endurance base building phase, minor damage occurs in the muscles. This damage is repaired and the muscle grows stronger, if sufficient recovery is allowed, which is the principle of Supercompensation. Alternating longer days at a slightly slower pace with shorter days at a slightly faster pace allows the athlete to make continuous progress. Therefore, do not do two tempo runs in a row; we allow at least 2 easier days in between tempo runs. If you are working on basic speed twice a week, such as repeat 40s one day and 200s another day, always allow at least 2 days between those sessions. As long as our athletes get sufficient sleep and a well balanced diet (and not running too fast every day), progress will continue.

Recovery becomes even more critical in the anaerobic phase. During this phase, a hard interval workout must be followed by a minimum of one day of easy running to allow the body to recover. In this phase, the risk of muscular "break down" is far higher, so caution is urged. When in doubt, allow for extra recovery, as necessary.

Some coaches use a dialog that goes something like this:

COACH: Do workouts make you better or worse?
ATHLETE: Better!
COACH: Then why don't you do a workout every day, and the day before your races?
ATHLETE: Because I'll be too tired and need to recover.
COACH: Thank you, case closed!

In simple terms, workouts break down the muscles. The benefit doesn't come until adequate recovery allows the muscles time to rebuild.

13. STRIDE RATE

Stride rate and stride frequency make very interesting topics. This is an area where all the aspects of training come together. We are looking for the quick stride rate of a sprinter, but we also must have great endurance in order to maintain stride length.

Stride rate is the number of individual foot strides the athlete takes in one minute. We measure it by right foot strikes times two. (Example: 90 right foot strikes x 2 = 180 stride rate per minute) The goal is to have athletes work towards a stride rate of 180 or higher.

Stride length is the distance of each stride. There are a variety of ways to define and measure stride length, but we will call it roughly the distance from the right foot strike to the left foot strike. Stride length is determined by factors such as leg length and leg strength, but can also be altered by flexibility and fatigue. All factors affecting stride length must be looked at carefully by the coach. A good example of the importance of stride length is: if an athlete loses 3 inches per stride, and is taking 180 strides per minute, we are looking at losing 540 inches per minute!

What is the stride length of an athlete who has a stride rate of 185, maintains an even stride rate and stride length for the entire race, and runs 1 mile in 5:00?

If Kenenisa Bekele has a stride rate of 200 and runs 10,000 meters in 26:17, what is his stride length?

Photo: Michael Grant, who Mick coached to multiple youth National Championships, also became a Massachusetts State Class Mile Champion. Here with the legendary multiple gold medalist and multiple world record setter Kenenisa Bekele. Bekele has an exceptionally high stride rate and stride length. **Courtesy photo,** Jossi Fritz-Mauer

Shorter runners will tend to have faster stride rates than taller runners, but taller runners will tend to have longer stride length. Each athlete will have his own optimal combination of stride rate and stride length, and we want to maximize each individual. We do want everyone to have a stride rate over 180.

What we want to do is strengthen the athlete, so he has the conditioning to maintain stride rate and stride length, and to increase stride length over time.

An area we need to pay attention to is lengthening stride. We do not make stride length gains by extending foot strike (where your foot hits the ground). DO NOT OVER STRIDE! Foot strike must always be directly beneath the hips, in order to avoid a braking action.

14. BASIC SPEED

Basic speed is very important for young middle distance and distance runners to develop. Our future best event will most likely be decided by our 200m time. Although we probably can't make a non-sprinter into a sprinter due to genetic limitations; we want to improve every athlete's basic speed as much as is possible. To do this, we need to work on it most of the year. Most coaches never actually work on the basic speed of middle and distance runners, and if you do, it will give your runners an advantage. This is what differentiates our coaching method and this book from other coaching methods and books. We work on endurance AND basic speed most of the year.

So why is basic speed important for a distance runner? Basic speed determines your ultimate potential in the middle and distance events, as we will explain in a moment. We have already established that endurance is the key to all middle and long distance events. In fact, building endurance is by far the most important component to improved performance and it must be the cornerstone of the year's training. Weight training also helps develop basic speed. This is covered in **Chapter 33**.

Let's consider an example of a young athlete with a goal to run 2:00 minutes for the 800m by senior year in high school. His current best 400m is 61 seconds. So based on simple math, this athlete will never be able to run 2:00 minutes for the 800m no matter how much endurance he develops until he improves his basic speed. We want to improve his 400m time to 55 seconds or better. Simultaneously, he needs to build his endurance so that he can run two 60 second 400m's back to back. Based on this example, it is clear that basic speed will limit what we are capable of as distance runners, particularly 800/1500 meter middle distance runners.

Another benefit to working on basic speed becomes more important the further the athlete progresses in the sport. To race successfully at higher levels, a crucial tool is to be able to finish a race with "a big kick" especially in championship races. To have a big kick requires, first and foremost, that we have more endurance than the other competitors, so we can run fast, even when tired, at the end of the race, and secondly, it requires good basic speed.

Excellent endurance prepares the athlete to run closer to their maximum basic speed at the end, when races are decided. Superior endurance allows athletes with average basic speed to frequently out kick athletes with above average basic speed. The key point is that endurance protects finishing speed.

However, even if you have superior endurance, and you can run close to your maximum speed at the end of a race, you may find that your basic speed is too slow to win the race, which is another important reason to develop basic speed. At the world class level, championship races from 1500 through 10000 are often won with a 51-53 last lap (57-59 for women). On the other side, great basic speed is worthless if we don't have the endurance to stay on the pace. Much more will be covered on this subject in the Race Tactics Section (**see Chapter 26**).

To work on basic speed we need to run fast. Some coaches believe hard anaerobic repeats on the track such as doing fast 8 x 400m is "speed work." That workout does not develop basic speed. Firstly, 400m is too far to run close to top speed. Secondly, so much lactic acid is produced; muscles never completely recover between intervals, so we can't run fast enough to stimulate the fast twitch muscle fibers enough for them to be forced to improve.

Some coaches believe by doing frequent "**strides**" or "striders" i.e. running 6-10 by 60-150 at 70% effort at the end of a daily distance run will develop speed. It is a great neuromuscular workout to keep runners fast twitch muscles in shape during the base phase and they should be used; however, they are run too slowly to stimulate any actual speed development. The end result is, many coaches think they are working on basic speed, but few actually are.

We need to run shorter distances, such as 40's, 50's, 70's, 100's, 150's or 200's. These should be done with a running or "**flying start**" to minimize injury risk, and should be done with the wind at your back. The first few should be slower than the last few to minimize injury risk. Also, they should rarely be run all out, even on the last one, as 90% effort is enough to stimulate improvement in basic speed. However, the last few reps must be run much faster than 70% effort (i.e. in the 85-90% range to stimulate basic speed development). Routine strides or striders won't accomplish that effect, especially when done after a distance training run.

Although fast running does produce lactic acid, we want to minimize it. The key, in this type of speed development work, is to allow sufficient rest between each interval, to allow our circulatory system to flush out the lactic acid, so that it doesn't accumulate, so we can continue to run fast and stimulate the fast twitch muscle fibers. That is why these workouts are called alactic training. The purpose of this workout is to work on basic speed, not **lactic acid tolerance,** which is done in the **anaerobic phase (see Chapter 10)**. These workouts have completely different purposes, and that must be clearly understood.

We use two primary workouts to improve basic speed. The first type of "Basic Speed" workout we use is 4-6 x **40m**. Walk back to the start for full recovery. We begin the first repetition at "medium-hard," and each subsequent sprint should be faster. **We stop as soon as the athlete's performance slips, which usually happens by the 4th, 5th or 6th rep.** This is an excellent way to improve basic speed during the base phase. It should be started a few weeks after a beginning runner starts training and used for many years, until diminishing returns are encountered. You obviously can vary and substitute other distances such as 50's, 70's, 100's or 150's, depending on how your particulate athlete responds to the training. Additionally, you can substitute short hill repeats of 4-6 x 20-70 meters with full recovery between each repeat or even use stadium stairs. As stated previously, ensure there are at least 2 days in between days you work on basic speed. Also, on days you work on basic speed, you perform any scheduled aerobic distance run AFTER the speed work, so they can run the speed workout fresh and fast. Alternately, you can separate the daily aerobic distance run and the speed by doing one in the AM and the other in the PM.

200s

This is an actual conversation:
Athlete: These 200's are too slow.
Coach Mick: They are at your goal race pace.
Athlete: I hear you telling me you don't want me to run fast!
Coach Mick: I'm telling you I want you to run fast on Saturday
(Actual result: Athlete ran a personal best 1:49.6)

We also use a second type of very gradual work that is a staple of our program for rhythm and sustained speed development, also known as **speed endurance**, and we use it in the base phase (i.e. most of the year), which is 5-8 x 200m with a 200 walk or 200 walk/jog or 200 jog recovery, depending on the age and fitness of the athlete. It trains the athlete to run relaxed at high speeds. This type of workout was used by Frank Gagliano, the great middle distance coach. For example, beginning in the fall, it is running relatively easy, somewhere between

35-40 seconds per 200m for our experienced 10-13 year olds, so they get used to the workout, and can maintain form for the full 200, get used to running fast, and learn pacing. Every few weeks, we will run them slightly faster on average, and eventually they are not only learning pace and rhythm and working on maintaining form at higher speeds, they are also working on improving basic sustained speed or speed endurance in the second half of the base phase. It is easy to see that by just gradually running a little faster every few weeks, that over the course of the year, we will be running much faster by summer, and improving sustained basic speed. Beginning runners should incorporate these into their weekly base phase training once a week, after they have reached the point they are comfortably capable of running them in 45 seconds or faster. Until that point, they should focus only on running repeat 40's as explained above and building endurance, until they can run comfortably run repeat 200's in 45 seconds or faster. Between each 200 there is a 200 recovery, and they should be fully recovered before the next 200. This is not an anaerobic interval workout. For beginning and very young athletes, this means a 200 walk. Over the years this for fitter and older athletes is a 100 walk followed by a 100 jog. Once the athlete becomes very fit, after many years of building endurance, they can jog the whole 200 and still be fully recovered, before they start the next one.

Photo: Mick Grant coached athlete Russell Brown, winning the High School 800 at the Maine Distance Festival, running for Mick Grant's Lynx Elite. **Courtesy photo, Alison Wade/New York Road Runners**

15. PEAKING AND TAPERING FOR THE TARGET RACE

We have now done the mileage for endurance, we have worked on basic speed to be fast, we have done our anaerobic workouts, to prepare our bodies to handle lactic acid, and we have done some pacing work or time trials or preparation races, and now we want to peak for the championship race.

Now that we have completed all of this training, we are ready to "polish our diamond". The peaking and tapering phase is mostly rest and sharpening. We pay very close attention to resting heart rate (HR) in this phase; to be sure our athlete is recovered. Frequently, after a rigorous training program, our athlete will have an elevated resting HR **(see Chapter 16 for more details on HR)**. In order to run at our best, we want the body to be rested, so we need to bring down this elevated resting heart rate. Rest and recovery should work wonders for bringing our resting heart rate down. The reason we want to bring our resting heart rate down now is simply to enable our athlete to race **FRESH**. In general, we will reduce total mileage volume by 20-30% over the last two weeks leading up to the most important race, depending on a number of factors including race distance, age, and health of athlete, and this freshens the athlete. The last long hard workout should be done 10 days before the championship. After that, workouts should be low in volume and fast; fast enough to get in oxygen debt, but short enough so the athlete recovers quickly in the days after the workout. **(See Chapter 11 to review sample peaking workouts.)**

For this "final polishing", we do some very short fast sprints. We will also run a small amount at our goal race pace. For example, during the last tapering week, leading up to a Saturday 800m race, we might run 6 or 8 x 50-70 meter accelerating sprints on Saturday and 4 x 200m **AT RACE PACE** on Wednesday. We want to be fresh, and we want to understand our pace. On race day, we want to compete well, and we want to be smart. Many good races are lost, because the athlete has become excited and gone out too fast. He may have done everything else correctly, but he didn't memorize his pace and execute his plan well.

16. HEART RATE

We use heart rate (HR) as a tool. We monitor **Training HR** as explained previously in **Chapters 8 and 9,** and we also measure **Resting HR**. It is useful to measure resting HR to monitor the health of the athlete. I like to monitor Resting HR to know if an athlete needs more rest. By rest, we don't mean taking days off completely, we mean doing relatively short, easy aerobic distance runs, until the athlete recovers. Short easy runs actually speeds recovery faster than complete rest, because it helps remove waste products from previous hard efforts, and increases blood flow in the muscles resulting in faster recovery. We use Training HR always on tempo runs and occasionally on easy runs and steady distance runs. This immediately shows if our athlete is running too hard.

Training HR Review:

120 or less   This effort is too slow to be effective for good aerobic development (i.e. jogging).

120-140   This effort is in the lower aerobic range and is fairly comfortable.

140-160   This effort is a solid effort in the middle of the aerobic range.

160-170   This effort is at the high end of the aerobic range (Tempo run) and is challenging.

170+   This effort is in the anaerobic range and is getting very hard.

Our kids will take HR for 10 seconds by putting their fingers on their neck the instant they complete a run and multiply by 6 to get the beats per minute. Alternately, you can wear a HR monitor.

Resting HR

One goal of training is to build a strong, efficient heart. A low resting HR reduces the workload on the heart. We want a low Resting HR and a high Stroke Volume. Remember that improvement only occurs during recovery which is the concept of Supercompensation. Therefore, planning enough recovery during training is crucial for improvement. Athletes should take Resting HR at the same time every day, preferably first thing in the morning.

An elevated Resting HR for more than one day can mean over-training, illness, or fatigue. If the athlete has an unusually elevated HR for several days, it is a good idea to back off training and get extra recovery. For example, if Resting HR is normally 50 and it measures 55 for several days, we want to plan some rest to get back to 50. If we don't pay attention, it could go from 55 to 60, then 65, etc, until the athlete breaks down from fatigue, injury, or illness. Resting HR should respond well to recovery days. Again, by recovery days we don't mean days off, we mean days of short easy aerobic runs. Over time, as the athlete becomes fitter, resting HR will get lower.

Resting HR will be elevated for two or three days sometimes, during harder stages of training. As the athlete learns about how their body responds to training, it will become easier to understand daily HR. There is a difference between elevated HR from training and elevated HR from over-training or illness. We manage wellness by allowing HR to be slightly elevated for a couple days during heavy training, and then bring it down with recovery. If HR doesn't respond to this recovery, plan on more recovery! It is important to understand that HR will fluctuate and that daily HR is a coaching tool. We like to bring resting HR down in the last two weeks leading up to target races. If you suspect overtraining or are trying to find the cause of poor performance, use resting HR as a valuable tool.

For our younger kids, 14 and under in particular, HR varies a lot. What we do with the younger kids is monitor how quickly HR is increasing over the course of a workout. If, for example, a girl's HR is increasing rapidly during a tempo run, we need to back off the pace a little and get the number stabilized. This method works with all athletes, but it is especially useful with younger kids who haven't developed a big aerobic base. Always watch how young kids are breathing and keep HR under 170.

Photo: Will Seidel, who was coached by Mick Grant. Seidel was part of Mick's Junior Olympic Champion and record setting 4 x 800 team. Like most of Mick's athletes, he had great range in high school, running 52.5 for 400, 1:56.00 for 800, and finished 2nd in the New England Private School XC Championships. **Courtesy photo, Cheryl Treworgy, prettysporty.com**

17.   FORM WORK

We want our athletes to run with the best form possible. Actually, we want them to be perfect!   We run tall and proud. Shoulders and arms must be relaxed. ("Hands through the pockets," as we learned from Frank Gagliano).   We do form drills almost every practice, for about 10 to 15 minutes. We look for efficiency. We want to eliminate wasteful movement.

- The top of the head and the hips are to be moving forward in as straight a line as possible.
- Eliminate any hip or shoulder twisting. All energy is to be used in moving forward.
- Arms move back and forth.   We do not want any flapping or flailing of arms.
- Keep everything relaxed. No energy sapping tightness in arms, shoulders, hands, face, etc.

"I want you to be smooth!"

Some high school and college teams will do much more work on drills.   The sequence we use is relaxed skipping, high knees, high knees bounding, "A" skips, "B" skips, butt kicks, and fast feet. What we are looking for is run tall and proud, hips tall, good arms (a.k.a. "hands through the pockets"), relaxed shoulders, "toe up, heel up, knee up" and light feet (like running over hot coals). We are teaching the kids to reduce ground contact time. We don't want to hear "bam, bam, bam" every step! Kids can and should understand this. We want the drills to be crisp, with quick repetition (practice high stride rate). We tell the kids to always run in a straight line and NEVER be sloppy. Good arm motion, hands and shoulders relaxed, drive elbows back. Nice tall posture is critical on all drills.

The sequence we use is **two to four times each of the first three drills**, for about 20-30 meters and two times for the last two drills for five seconds each, all on grass.

- ✓ **SKIPPING**   Exactly what it says, nice and relaxed, to get loose
- ✓ **HIGH KNEES**   We're running with an exaggerated knee lift. Maintain run tall posture. Do not lean back.
- ✓ **HIGH KNEES BOUNDING**   For this drill, we want to drive off hard and drive the knee up, get some air! It is important to maintain tall posture and efficient arm use.

- ✓ **"A" and "B" SKIPS** Developed by Gerard Mach, a former sprint coach in Canada. We teach these drills by walking through them until the technique is learned. Good, tall posture and good arm motion, as always, is very important. Athletes will feel themselves up on the balls of their feet while performing these drills. On the "A" drill, we will focus on knee lift, but are looking at developing excellent "toe up, heel up, knee up" action in a nice, crisp skipping action. On the "B" drill, we add a foreleg extension and powerful, efficient foot strike, in a good toe up position, right below the hips. Stride length will be very short.
- ✓ **BUTT KICKS** Run tall, very short steps, kick heels up, just like it says
- ✓ **FAST FEET** Run as tall as possible, as high repetition as possible, "Pick 'em up and Put 'em down"

There are many good videos available online for learning running drills.

We want our athletes to be smooth and efficient. Form drills are a useful way both for the athletes to work on running mechanics and for coaches to inspect every athlete. Over time, working on form drills improves a runner's efficiency. We also want to be sure our athletes are working hard on getting their knees up. Whether racing at cross country or on the track, once an athlete fatigues, he loses the nice knee lift and crucial stride length. We want our athletes to have knee lift ingrained into their brains. Sometimes, we run through our form drills on a hill, so knee lift becomes even more important. High knees, bounding and striding are much more difficult on a hill than on a flat surface. Some coaches even bring their athletes to stadium to run through repeat "stadium steps". Working on knee lift is working on power.

18. INTENSITY
MOVING TO THE NEXT LEVEL

The most important thing for coaches to remember is that running needs to be fun. That does not mean that the kids can't work hard, and it doesn't mean that the kids should be goofing off at practice. It does mean that running should be enjoyable and rewarding. Athletes should understand that running is something that can be enjoyed over an entire lifetime as part of a healthy lifestyle. Our experience suggests that kids suffer "burnout" from too much anaerobic interval work and from over-racing (INTENSITY DENSITY).

Burnout seems to be caused by a bad balance between intensity and fitness. If the key to long term success is having some fun and staying healthy, athletes, parents and coaches must carefully monitor the volume of intensity relative to the athlete's age, training history, level of fitness and other factors. Most young athletes should be running at least 90% of training volume aerobically or 95% of training days.

Our experience has shown that kids do not suffer from burnout from aerobic endurance training. This may be in part because it is not too intense or physically stressful. The larger reason is possibly that kids enjoy going on aerobic distance runs with other kids. The kids can talk, enjoy the scenery on the trails, and help each other push their aerobic development. There is definitely a bonding that develops within training groups. Far from burnout, the kids actually look forward to coming to practice. Kids have fun improving.

At some point, most kids will be ready to move up the next level of intensity. There are many levels of intensity, and moving up to the next level should always be done carefully. Improving is often compared to climbing a ladder. Every step is great, but there is always another step on the way to the top. Climb the ladder one rung at a time.

The first two rules must still be obeyed.
1. **Have Fun   They must be enjoying what they are doing.**
2. **Stay Healthy The athlete needs to stay healthy.**

The athlete needs to always be part of any decision to move up to the next level. This will be more rigorous training, including:

mileage, faster pace, more competitive races, etc. At each higher level, there is more responsibility on the part of the athlete. I think the coach should always have a 100% commitment to the long term development of the athlete, and the athlete needs to make a higher level of commitment with each step to the next level.

As the athlete moves up each level in intensity, we use resting HR slightly more to monitor recovery. It is important always to remember that we want to keep the athlete healthy. We will allow resting HR to remain at a slightly higher than normal level for several weeks during heavy training, as long as it does not continue climbing. We want to keep an eye out that the athlete is getting enough recovery to prevent injury and illness. Leading up to target races and during scheduled recovery weeks, we will bring the resting HR back down through additional rest.

A very important consideration for coaches and athletes is to use extreme caution and care when bringing an athlete up to the next level of intensity. We have seen too many examples of athletes moving along too quickly. For example, a 9th grade phenom may be a terrific athlete, but this is still a 14 year old kid, who needs to build a solid foundation. Resist the temptation to bring athletes along too rapidly.

19. KEYS TO SUCCESS

1) Consistency - Consistency in training is the key to success in middle and distance running. No amount of intermittent bursts of hard work will trump an athlete who trains consistently year round. To reach your full potential you need to be coming close to training 7 days a week year round. As discussed earlier in the book, some kids are not mentally ready for this type of commitment, and they should be gradually directed towards this goal as their enthusiasm for the sport increases over time. As pointed out by Arthur Lydiard, an athlete who runs 6 days a week will be 15% less prepared than an athlete of equal talent who runs 7 days a week. An athlete who takes the winter off will be 25% less prepared than a year round runner, and an athlete who takes the summer and winter off will be 50% less prepared. An athlete who does periodic killer workouts and bursts of big mileage intermixed with lots of days off and extended lay-offs, will not be able to compete with an athlete of equal talent, who runs every day following sound principles.

2) Patience - Patience is critical for success in middle and distance running. Almost every Olympic and Word Championships medalist in the middle distances and distances in the modern era spent 14 to 16 years of training before they won their medal. This includes the occasional 20 year old African champion, who started running several miles to and from school each day from age 6 onwards, to the Americans or Europeans, who start running at age 14, and became champions in their mid to late 20s. The reason is it takes years of building endurance to get anywhere near your full potential, so it is important for the coach and athlete to have a long term patient attitude towards running. Also, improvement is rarely in a straight line, despite the best training. There should be steady improvement from year to year, but it won't be a straight line up. There will be breakthroughs or times of rapid improvement, but there will also be plateaus where despite a sound program, you go a few months with little apparent progress. This is where patience is key to keep training and wait for the next improvement.

3) Focus on Endurance Building Most of the Year - The goal of the athlete and coach is to be significantly better next year than this year. The only way to accomplish this is to focus on endurance building most of the year. You want to minimize the racing periods and the

anaerobic interval periods leading up to the racing periods such that you are spending 9 months or more in endurance base building - running aerobic miles every day, weekly Long Runs and 1-2 weekly sub threshold tempo runs. Remember, running aerobic miles is putting money in the bank and races and anaerobic interval training is taking money out of the bank. Just as with money and the power of compound interest, endurance can be built to levels you never thought were possible for a given athlete.

4) Persistence - Every medalist suffered injuries and illness, setbacks in running, setbacks when life interferes with running, and many bad races. They became champions, because every time a setback occurred, they persisted and overcame what set them back, and they persevered onward. After the setback, they analyzed their training and lifestyle to determine the cause of the setback, and made adjustments aimed to prevent recurrence of the same setback. This is yet another reason why we recommend keeping a training journal. All runners get knocked for a loop at times, and you have to pull yourself back up, and work to get back to where you were, and then move on to new higher level.

5) Work on Basic Speed most of the Year - As we pointed out earlier, it is your basic speed that will ultimately limit how far you can go in the middle distances, and to a less extent, in the distances. That is why it is critical that you work to improve your speed most of the year. Again we are NOT talking about anaerobic interval training to sharpen for races; that does nothing to improve basic speed. We are also not talking the run of the mill "strides" most people do. These are great for neuromuscular fitness and maintenance, but the way most people do them won't improve basic speed. You need to be doing 3-10 repeats of 40 to 200 meters with near full recovery, and running them fast enough to stimulate an improvement in basic speed. Just as the best thing for running endurance is to do endurance running and not swimming or cycling, the best thing for running speed is to run fast. Occasionally you can substitute 3-6 short hard hill sprints with full recovery, as they will also improve speed.

6) Toughness - To be successful, toughness is critical, which is why we point it out as a key to success, but it is difficult to coach or teach or to develop. Toughness seems to be more an innate quality a person possesses and/or is learned at a very young age, well before one enters

the sport, so it is difficult for a coach to improve this area of the runner. There are two types of toughness, a subtle type that is much more valuable, and the overt type that is valuable but not critical. You will encounter athletes who possess neither type, one type but not the other, and the rare athlete who possesses both. The subtle type of toughness is the ability to be consistent in training and always run (barring injury/illness), regardless of how busy you are, the weather conditions, how you feel, what is going on in your life, and other outside influences. This type of toughness will give you the consistency in your training to easily overcome runners with superior genetic talent. The coach can explain this, praise this, direct this, and foster an environment conducive for this, so the athlete can improve this area over time. The overt toughness is the ability to gut out and take on the extraordinary pain of lactic acid in the middle and late stages of a race. This type of toughness almost always decides who wins a very close race. This area is difficult to improve, but can be improved a little, as the athlete becomes fitter and more confident over time. The good news is that an athlete does not have to possess super toughness to become a champion. As long as they possess at least average toughness, they can simply train 1% better than the super tough guys and beat them. Runners who posses below average toughness are frustrating to coach, because they will often quit when the going gets tough in a race, but all is not lost, because with proper training, they too can simply get better and better, year after year, and while their races will often be disappointing, they will be running against a higher level of competition and running faster times every year.

7) Ability to Improvise – Nothing ever goes exactly as planned. Therefore, when unplanned events happen, the coach and athlete cannot use these inevitable events as an excuse to not train. There are too many examples to give, but here are a few. In bad weather, plan on running early or later in the day to avoid the bad weather, if possible. If not possible, run in the bad weather or on a treadmill or run in place inside, if necessary.

If you plan to workout on the track, and it is covered in snow or ice, or a soccer game or track meet is going on, always have a back-up plan, and do the workout on a wheeled off or measured section of flat road, or even a treadmill, as a last resort. Keep doing your basic speed training in the winter. If the outdoor track is covered in snow and ice, use a wheeled off flat stretch of road with good sun exposure, that is clear of ice and snow. If weather is too bad to do a tempo or workout, move it forward or backwards a day, and instead do easy distance on the bad weather day. If you have a big work or school or family event or are traveling, get up early to get your run in. The bottom line is if there is a will, there is a way.

Photo: Mick Grant coached athlete Keely Maguire at the Boston Indoor Games High School Elite Mile. Maguire's long list of accomplishments is listed with an earlier photo in the book. Maguire followed all the keys for success. **Courtesy photo, Victah Sailer/photorun.net**

D. RACING , IMPROVEMENT MATTERS

20. RACES

The goal in selecting races is quality over quantity.

- Move up your race distance gradually, as you develop endurance. Start youth athletes racing at the sprints, literally 100 and 200, and gradually move them up to the 400. Do this even though you are constantly building up their endurance. Don't make the mistake most parents and youth coaches make, of instantly having kids run 5K and 10K road races, even if they are very good at it. This is putting the cart before the horse, and stunting their long term potential in the sport, by rushing into longer distances. In cross country, limit them to 2K or 4K races, until they are high school age. In high school, do not run further than 5K for cross country. On the track, Mick's rule was no one could move up past the 800, until they could break 2:20. Regardless, on the track, no youth runner should be doing any track races longer than a mile, until they reach high school age.

- Every race must have a specific purpose. Don't race just because there is one on the calendar.

- Always remember you get better by training, not running meaningless races. Racing is an opportunity to execute a plan you have prepared yourself for in training.

- Legitimate reasons for races are:

- End of Cross Country or Track season "championship" race that YOU are qualified for.

- One of the few (i.e. 2-5) races leading up to the "championship" that you will use as developmental races and/or qualifying races, following months of solid base phase training.

- Have long-term and short-term goals---both are very important.

- Short-term goals lead in the direction of long term goals.

- Always have a specific race plan - usually a specific time goal and/or approximate place goal you are trying to achieve. Never go into a race without a plan.

- Don't worry about where you are at right now. Improvement matters!

- Break down races into splits (i.e. 200m) so you know what to work on.
- Always work on running even splits (i.e. the same pace the whole way) or slightly negative splits (i.e. running the 2nd half of the race faster). Don't go out too fast. The coach should be giving splits and keeping the runner on pace whenever possible. The runner needs to adjust their pace at each split, by either speeding up, or slowing down to stay on pace.
- Gradually, work on improving each split. Learn to run negative splits.
- Whether racing track or cross-country, practice race pace sometimes.
  (Ex., if our goal is to run 6 minute mile pace for 5k, practice 1 mile tempos at goal pace. When we get stronger, run up to 1.5 miles at goal pace.)
- Be patient and realistic -- the only thing that matters is gradual improvement.
- We recommend starting with short races as a young athlete (100m, 200m).
- Ask to run on relays. Relays are both excellent speed training and fun.

Photo: April O'Brien, who was part of Mick's DMR team that won the Dartmouth Relays versus college teams and was part of the Lynn Woods Relay setting team. She also ran a 2:18 800 and 2:57 1000 in high school and ran at Dartmouth College.
Courtesy photo, Lynx Elite Athletics/Bob O'Brien

21. SETTING GOALS

The coach and athlete must discuss and establish short term, intermediate term, and long term goals. It is important that both coach and athlete agree on these goals. The goals may have to be periodically adjusted, based on actual results or other circumstances.

Long term goals are usually at least 2-4 years out. An example may be a high school freshman, who runs 800m currently in 2:15, wanting to break 2 minutes for 800m, or a top ten finish in a championship cross country race, by his senior year. An intermediate goal for the same freshman may be to run a 2:10 800m by the end of the freshman year. A short term goal may be to run 2:14 in next week's race.

There are certain rules to follow when setting goals. They need to be challenging, yet within the ability of the runner. Setting unrealistic goals, either too high or too low, will do the runner no good. Setting goals too high results in discouragement and disillusionment for the runner and can sour the love for the sport by the athlete. Setting goals too low are also no good, because the athlete won't be inspired by them to achieve their potential. Being able to set appropriate, realistic goals, relies on experience, a clear understanding of the sport, being positive and ambitious, but grounded in reality. Needless to say, a new coach and new runner may have trouble establishing appropriate goals, and we may have to adjust them as time goes on. The skill will come from experience and understanding of the sport, for both coach and athlete.

Some of the factors to consider in intermediate and long term goal setting include evaluating the athlete's age, gender, basic speed, build, current best times, annual progression, training history, past response to training, future planned training, injury history, and the athlete's level of enthusiasm and dedication. Needless to say, this is no easy task, with so many factors to consider. Having goals that the coach and athlete both understand is important, because goals help bring meaning to training and help define progress.

For short term goals, a different set of factors come into play, including recent race times, recent training; is our athlete still in the midst of heavy training or are we tapered and fresh? The level of competition, weather conditions, the relative importance of the race, expected race pace and our athlete's strategy for the race, are also factors. As stated previously, having athletes practice goal race pace plays an important part in assessing progress relative to goals. An appropriate short term goal might be running slightly faster than last week. Short term goals should be attainable quickly.

Setting goals is important, and should not be taken lightly. Setting higher goals presumes a higher commitment. We want to use short term goals as small steps towards our more ambitious long term goals. This is the safest way for our athlete to move in the direction they desire. As discussed in **Chapter 18**, moving up to the next level will be more physically challenging. Training to run a 2:00 800 is more demanding, than training to run a 2:15 800, so expect it, and want it!

Photo: Eric McDonald, who was coached by Mick Grant. Like most athletes Mick coached, he had great range running a 1:58 800, 2:30 1000 and 4:19 mile, and was a Massachusetts State Class XC Champion. Later, at UMass-Lowell, he ran a 4:07 mile and 8:14 3000 (worth 8:53 2 mile), was an NCAA All American in track and qualified for the NCAA XC championships multiple times.
Courtesy photo, Chip Bott

22. LEARNING PACING

Learning proper pacing is critical to be successful at racing. Interestingly, the younger the level of competition, the more critical pacing becomes. The nearly universal tendency, in youth athletics, is to go out too fast in all races. As legendary coach Bill Bowerman once said, "No mile race has ever been won in the first 200, but many have been lost in the first 200 by going out too fast." University of Colorado coach Mark Wetmore, who has coached numerous NCAA team and individual cross country champions, instills in his runners to not make **The Big Mistake** of going out too fast. They understand that the real racing is done in the second half of the race. The problem many young athletes have with pacing is confidence. It takes a lot of confidence to make a conscious decision to go out behind and "stalk" the competition, with a plan of racing the second half. Everyone likes to be out in front. An example of this confidence and control is Coach Joe Newton's York High School teams in Elmhurst, Illinois, which have ranked number one in the country many times. In State Championships, Coach Newton's runners stay in their starting box after the gun is fired and count quickly to three before starting. This ensures they start out behind the field and won't go out too fast. They have won over 25 state titles in Illinois.[2] A simple strategy that works well in almost all circumstances is to ignore everyone else and run your own race, and stay on your goal pace for the first 75% of the race, and then in the last 25% of the race, focus on racing and beating any runners near you.

Coaches must teach athletes to be aggressive AND smart. If we have a plan, execute the plan. For example, an eager young miler wants to run under 4:40 and runs the first 400m of a mile in 63. Our boy then gradually slows, runs the last 400m in 80, and has a final time of 4:45. This is a painful lesson in pacing. In the next race, our eager young miler learns his lesson and goes out in 68. He does a much better job in holding the pace and finishes with a 4:35. He went out 5 seconds slower, but finished 10 seconds faster. That was a lesson well learned.

---

[2] Coaching Cross Country Successfully by Joe Newton, Human

Kinetics, pg 86

A cursory examination of World Records in middle and long distance events over the last 100 years reveals that the bulk of the records were set by running an even pace. The longer the race, the more the more important it is to not go out too fast and "run positive splits". Most records in the longer distances were set with even pacing or slightly **"negative splits"**, meaning running the second half of the race faster than the first half of the race. Coach Newton considers an ideal race for his top runner is to run the first mile in 5:10, the second mile in 5:00 and the last mile in 4:55, with the last 300 meters run "with reckless abandon".[2] Many runners do just the opposite and run the first 300 meters with reckless abandon, and they kill their race.

The ideal for the 800m is splitting the first 400m 2-3 seconds faster than the second 400m. For example, to run 1:59 in the 800, it might be good to run 58-59 for the first 400m and 60-61 for the second half. Far too many runners attempt to break 2:00 by running 55 for the first 400m, then fade badly on the second 400m, and fall short of their goal. For the 400, the ideal is to run the first 200 2.0 to 2.5 seconds faster than the 2nd 200. For all distances over 800, you want to run even or slightly negative splits. As Frank Gagliano said; "If you don't run evenly, someone else will, and they'll beat you."

There is no salvation for an athlete who goes out too fast in a race, so it should be avoided at all cost. You cannot recover in any way; you can only hope to settle in and hang on the best you can. The good news is you can recover from going out too slowly by running **negative splits**. As stated above, the problem of going out too fast is more common at the youth level, so if we teach our athletes proper pacing, it affords our athletes a huge advantage.

So how do we teach proper pacing?

In Practice: As explained in **Chapter 14**, during the base phase, which is most of the year for our athletes, we work on basic speed, and once a week, we do repeat 200's with full recovery. In addition to being useful for improving sustained speed, 200's are useful for learning pace and rhythm, so the athlete gets used to running smoothly at progressively faster speeds. Running 200's gives the kids very good practice at learning pacing. In tempo runs, we also give splits, so again the runner is constantly learning a full range of paces, and eventually most develop a built in clock to recognize various paces.

When we race, all the pacing practice we have done comes together with the aerobic endurance training to produce great results.

In Races: As explained above, we break each track race down into 200m sections and the coach or others give the runners splits to keep them on pace. In XC races, if practicable, you can wheel off the first 400 and 800 and give splits there and at the mile to make sure the athlete doesn't go out too fast and ruin their race.

Photo of some of Mick's athletes from left to right: Michael Grant, John Gillespie, Will Seidel, Russell Brown, and Joe Comeau. The accomplishments of Grant, Gillespie, Seidel, and Brown are described in other photos in the book. **Courtesy photo, Lynx Elite Athletics**

23. HOW MANY RACES IN ONE SEASON?

Each season we want to pick the 1 or 2 races that are the target race or races for the season. For our young athletes, or athletes who are running for a club and not their high school, it may be the Junior Olympic Cross Country Nationals in the fall, and the Hershey National Track & Field Championships or Junior Olympic National Track & Field Championships in the summer. If your athletes are not ready or able to compete at that level, select a local late season cross country race that would be a good fit for them and a local track meet in the late spring or early summer, where they can compete.

If you are competing for your high school, and you are not yet competitive on the statewide level, you want to pick your final 2 meets of the season you will be running in, such as an invitational JV XC race, the final dual meet, or your league championship. If you are competitive on a statewide level, you want to pick your state district and state final as your two races. If you happen to be competitive on a national level, you pick the Footlocker Regional and Footlocker Final. You do the same thing for the track season.

Once we determine our target races, how many races should we run per season? The most important thing we can say is do not over-race kids. There are a variety of reasons. Racing is meant to be fun and satisfying, and why we ultimately do the training. However, keep in mind, hard racing is always anaerobic, and as covered previously, puts a lot of stress on the Central Nervous System. The high school system in the United States has a demanding structure, apparently modeled after other team sports. Many high school athletes run 30 to 50 races in 9 months. Some athletes are often called to compete in two or three events at meets, which results in cases of young kids running close to 100 races in a single school year. With so many races, there leaves little time for proper training and recovery, which inhibits long term development, and can mentally and physically burn out athletes, and sour their love for the sport. Most colleges reduced the number of competitions, in order to allow athletes to train well. For example, many top college distance programs in the country don't have their middle and distance runners run their first indoor competition until late January or early February, while the typical younger, less conditioned high school athlete, may have already run several races by that point.

Remember, endurance training is putting money in the bank. Racing and anaerobic training is taking money out of the bank. We are interested in long term development; pick and choose races wisely. So what is an ideal number of races?

Some considerations include:

- Race Distance - Generally, the longer our race distance (ex. 2 mile or XC), the fewer the number of races.
- Athlete's Experience - More experienced runners can afford to run fewer races and spend more time training, whereas less experienced runners may need slightly more developmental race experience, but not much more.
- Conditioning - Generally, we do want to run a few races, prior to the target race. These races should be considered part of your preparation for your target races. They co-ordinate, or bring together, the aerobic and anaerobic training of the athlete, so we can achieve our best. In most cases, our athlete cannot run their best, without having a couple races under their belt. There are no one minute rest periods in the middle of a race, so interval training alone is not enough; we need to first do interval training and then co-ordination training. If no suitable races are available, we can use time trials in place of races.

Considering the above factors, we would consider 3-5 races appropriate for cross country, and 3-6 races each for indoor track and outdoor track. In track, a two miler might only run 2 or 3 races at the distance, plus 1 or 2 one mile races. A miler might run 3 one mile races, 1 two mile and 1 or 2 800's. An 800m runner may run 3 races at 800m, plus 1 or 2 400m races and possibly a one mile race. It is sometimes wise to skip a full indoor track season, and just work on building endurance and basic speed, during the winter, and maybe 1 or 2 indoor races to break things up.

It is easy for the club coach to pick the target races, and pick a few more races before the target races, and start the anaerobic phase/race phase the ideal 4-6 weeks before the target race.

The job of the high school coach is much, much harder, almost daunting. Most are faced with 10-16 meet XC, 10-15 meet indoor and 12-16 meet outdoor schedules and expectations from uninformed athletes, AD's, and parents and even fellow coaching staff members, who expect your middle and distance runners to run and run all out in all of those 32-50 meets, and win as many as possible, and score as many points as possible, and even to have your middle and distance runners double and even triple in some track meets, to squeeze every last point they can get out of the athlete. These uniformed people looking over your shoulder don't understand middle and distance running, and they think it is just like any other team sport, such as football or soccer, and they have no understanding and no interest in long term development of athletes, and to them the only thing that matters is next Tuesday's dual meet. I am sure a lot of you high school coaches are reading this and shaking your heads and saying "yes, been there, done that". So what is a high school middle distance/distance coach who is interested in actual long term development of their athletes supposed to do, when confronted with such ridiculous schedules, and all these outside (and sometimes inside) forces working against them? John Molvar provides a pie in the sky long term fix to this problem in **Chapter 26**.

How to Apply the Principles of This Book, While Dealing With the Excessive High School Race Schedule

So what is the high school coach supposed to do in the meantime? What the coach needs to do takes innovation, courage, patience, and confidence, so it is not going to be easy. You basically have to forsake the entire first two thirds or three quarters of the meets each season, and instead of running all out in those, use them as part of training as follows:

1) First eliminate any meets from your schedule in your power that you can eliminate.

2) Determine the 2 most important meets of your season. For very low level teams, this could be the final dual meet versus your "traditional rival" and your league meet. For mid-level teams, it is your league meet and state district meet. For high level teams, this is the state district and statewide meet. For elite teams, this is the statewide meet and the Team Nationals.

3) Once you determine your final most important meet per step 2, count back about 6 weeks from that race, and mark that date on your calendar. That **key date** becomes the dividing line between the end of your Base Phase and the beginning of your Anaerobic/Race Phase.

4) You should do no anaerobic interval training prior to that key date. You should be working on building endurance via mileage, Long Runs, and tempo runs, as explained in earlier chapters in the book (see **Chapters 8 and 9**). You should also be working on basic speed 1-2 days a week as explained in **Chapter 14**.

5) Any races scheduled prior to that key date (and for most teams this will be half or three quarters of all meets on the schedule), should be

treated as tempo runs. This is obviously the hard part; because depending on the level of your team, you will lose some (relatively meaningless in the big picture) meets that you could have won. This is where you have to educate your athletes and deal with parents and AD's who won't understand. They need to know you are aiming for long term development of each athlete, and are trying to peak for the most important races at the end of the season.

6) You must "**train through**" all races prior to the key date, by not resting prior to races and keeping mileage up.

7) Once you reach the key date (which is about 6 weeks before your final most important race), choose 4 or 5 of the remaining races on the schedule for XC (and 4-7 races for track), that your runners will run all out in. Any additional races during this time should be used as tempo runs.

8) After the key date, you begin anaerobic interval training (**see Chapter 10**) and taper for the final 2 races.

8) Many of the top programs nationwide are using a similar method as described above. After a couple of years, your program will improve significantly, due to this long term approach, and in the short run, you will perform much better in the final, most important races of each season. What you sacrifice is the early (and generally meaningless) races. You will also get grumblings from some athletes, parents, etc. The beauty of this approach is that after a couple of years of this long term approach, your teams will be significantly better, and you can start winning meaningless dual meets, even with your runners using tempo effort in the early races. Obviously for the elite teams, recruiting kids to come out for the team is critical (and outside the scope of this book), and having them developing a solid summer mileage base is critical. However if the elite programs have one secret, it was just given away.

KEY POINTS
- Aerobic endurance training puts money in the bank.
- Anaerobic interval training takes money out of the bank, but is important in the peaking phase of training.
- Racing takes money out of the bank.
- If we keep taking money out of the bank, and don't put any back in, we will soon be broke!

Photo below of Mick's Club: back row Joe Comeau, Russell Brown, Mick Grant, John Gillespie, Michael Grant, front row Kaitlyn Wallace, Ashley Moulton, Robin Colt, Natasha Stevenson, Katie Dlesk   The accomplishments of Brown, Michael Grant, and Dlesk are listed with other photos in the book. Gillespie became a New England High School Champion and High School All American in the 4 x 800, and he later ran for Colgate University. Moulton was a multiple Hershey Massachusetts State Champion and Hershey National Regional sprint Champion and finalist at the Hershey Nationals. She went on to become an NCAA All American at UMass-Lowell and multiple New England Champion and school record setter. Stevenson was a Hershey Nationals finalist in the 4 x 100. Comeau was a Hershey's and Junior Olympics National finalist in the sprint relays and finished 2nd in the Mayor's Cup youth XC race. **Courtesy photo, Lynx Elite Athletics**

24. IMPORTANCE OF VARYING RACE DISTANCES

It is important to vary the race distances during the track season. There are several advantages to this including keeping the athlete mentally fresh and enthusiastic. Many athletes will get bored running the one mile 5 races in a row. Some athletes, who have a history of running the same distance every race, may even become afraid to try different events. You never want your athletes to fear anything related to competition including running over and under distances. Most athletes with long careers eventually move up in their primary race distance as they approach their full potential. We want our athletes to have the confidence and desire to race different distances. Varying race distances in the weeks leading up to the target race, leads to an improved performance. We recommend running races both shorter and longer, than the primary event, also known as **"Racing Over and Under"**. Shorter races prepare the body for the faster pace they will need to eventually run in the longer race. The longer races prepare the body for distance. This variation in early races is what Lydiard called **co-ordination training** and is a critical element in his philosophy. There are also psychological factors. Often a good strategy is to have the final race before the target race, be at a shorter distance. This helps make the pace feel easier for our athlete in their main event. Included below is a chart that you can use to compare races performances over different distances:

Conversion Chart to Compare Performances over Various Race Distances

To Convert From This Race Distance:	To this Race Distance:	Take Time In Seconds And Multiply by:
200	100	0.500
400	200	0.448
400	300	0.718
300	300 yards	0.900
500	400	0.771
600	400	0.598
600	500	0.797
800	400	0.427
800	600 yards	0.635
600	600 yards	0.890
800	600	0.714
1000	800	0.768
1000 yards	800	0.850
mile	800	0.450
mile	1200	0.720
mile	1500	0.925
mile	1600	Subtract 1.6 seconds
2 mile	mile	0.465
2 mile	3000	0.926
2 mile	3000 steeple	1.000
2 mile	3200	Subtract 3.2 seconds
5000	mile	0.290
5 mile	8000	Subtract 10 seconds
10000	5000	0.480
10000	5 mile	0.797
10 mile	10000	0.600
marathon	10000	0.214
marathon	Half marathon	0.465

25. WHY KIDS LOVE RELAYS

Photo: Indoor DMR team of Alanna Poretta, Keara Thomas, Emily Foster and Alison Travers. Poretta's accomplishments are detailed in an earlier photo. Keara was 4 time ISL and New England Champion in cross country, Conference Steeplechase Champion in college, and qualified for the USATF Nationals in the Steeple. Foster won a League XC championship and Travers became an ISL and New England Champion. **Courtesy photo, Lynx Elite Athletics/Jim Kobler**

Relay teams are an excellent method for building a team. Kids love relays. Some people may say track isn't a team sport, but most kids improve faster when training with a group of athletes with similar goals. Developing a relay team provides incentive for all team members to work hard. Kids do not like to let each other down. Being on a relay team is a "Badge of Honor" that kids wear proudly. Other members of your team will work hard to try to make a relay team.

    The total is greater than the sum of its parts. That is a good description of what relay teams can be. We see many kids run personal best times on relays. We think this is due to the close bond teammates develop and the pride they have in each other. This bond creates an energy that enhances the training environment and is very exciting to be a part of.

26. PICKING RACES

Selecting the races we want to compete at is easy in theory, but difficult in practice. It is easy to say that we want to run the Conference Championship, the State Championship, and the National Championship, but the fact is we need to work within the system we have, and race at an appropriate level for the athlete. There are also fun meets, like relay meets, and invitational meets, that are appealing. We need to exercise discipline and caution in selecting which, and how many races, young athletes should compete at.

The plan should be completed before the season begins. If a coach wants to be successful, they must PLAN. The first step is deciding the most important target race. From that point, count the number of weeks until that race. We want to train well for as many weeks as possible, in order to have well prepared athletes. If we have a large team, some kids will have different target races than others. That is ok; it is all part of the planning process. A good coach is a prepared coach.

Once we have picked the target race, and we know how many weeks until that date, the next step is to periodize the available weeks in order to maximize training. We want to spend as much time as possible in the aerobic endurance base phase, but we want to cover all aspects of training.

As previously described in **Chapter 21**, High school coaches face huge obstacles with the current system. At many schools, there is nearly non-stop racing scheduled from early-September to mid-June. A common week has 2 races plus anaerobic interval training. **If the kids take an easy day before and after competitions, this scenario would have three hard days and four recovery days.** When is any time left for aerobic base building, which is the key to long term development? In **Chapter 21,** Coach Molvar provides the innovative high school coach a way to work around this terrible system. Later in **Chapter 26,** Coach Molvar offers a pie in the sky plan to reform the current high school system to be more suitable to long term development of middle and long distance runners.

Now that we have our target race and the number of weeks to prepare a periodized training schedule, we can fill it in with a small number of preparation races for our target race. We should find good competition and fun meets. We don't believe in just going to a competition, because someone is having a meet that day. There must be a good reason for every race we do. Ask yourself, what do we want to accomplish at this meet?

Remember, while you are racing, someone else is training. Choose wisely.

Photo: Katharina Eidmann, who was coached by Mick Grant. Kat became a Massachusetts State Champion in the 1000. **Courtesy photo, Lynx Elite Athletics/Michael Eidmann**

27. RACE PSYCHOLOGY; POSITIVE THINKING
AVOIDING PRE-RACE ANXIETY

"I've done all the work, put in my miles, stayed healthy and done the drills. Now I'm afraid that I won't run well in my championship. What will I do? What will people think about me?"
This is called "**Performance Anxiety**" and it is common. It is time to re-focus.

STRIVE FOR THE FOLLOWING
- Set appropriate race goals, then train and race accordingly.
- Reflect back on training. Training will indicate that we can run our goal time, so there is nothing to fear. Race hard and at the proper pace. In fact, the hard part (i.e. the training) is done. We have done the training, have appropriate goals, and know our race pace. The race is the reward.
- Aspire to achieve gradual improvement. It is critical to focus on one's own improvement and not what others are doing.
- In races, do not focus on competitors. You can't control them. Focus on yourself. Execute your race plan, and then race your competitors late in the race.
- Prepare to run YOUR best. You can only control yourself. See how fast YOU can run today!
- Be excited for the opportunity to run championships. This is one of the reasons you train so hard. Take advantage of your opportunities to run fast. You want to run fast; everyone wants to run fast RIGHT?? - This is good! Go out there and execute your plan, run as fast as you can, and go home happy, regardless of what place you finish.
- Don't fear your competition. Love your competition! Let them help you improve. Wish everyone well, and be excited that you all can run fast today. Always thank your competitors.
- **Athletes, coaches, parents and fans must always stay calm.** Racing requires confidence and focus. We want the athletes to execute their plan.
Confidence is contagious and so is nervousness.

"How to":

- **Stay positive**

  We do not criticize kids when they run poorly. We know how hard running is, and it doesn't always go as planned. We have all experienced a bad race.

- **Keep it fun**

  Remember Rule #1: Have Fun! We train well and practice to run specific times in specific events. There is no pressure. We have been consistent; we have set realistic goals for each athlete, based on a number of factors. When we go to race, we simply execute the plan. It will be hard, but that is the fun part. Pushing oneself to accomplish what we have not done before is fun!

- **Motivate without pressure**

  This should not be an issue. Athletes don't need to be motivated and they don't need to be pressured. Racing is simply executing a plan. If our athletes have trained well, we don't need to motivate them. If anything, motivating speeches are just a form of external pressure. We want to stay focused on our plan and execute it.

- **Analyze performances without being critical.**

  With our kids, they know the goal time, and if they don't hit it, they know they didn't run as well as expected. Nothing negative needs to be said. If they went out too fast, we will want to talk about a correction. We will point that out to them. We can do it in front of the team, if they happen to be around, so all can benefit. We never do it in a demeaning or negative way; it is education and the kids have no problem with it. In fact, when it does happen, they come up to me and admit they went out too fast, before we even say anything. The kids understand that and respect that. We don't believe that race analysis should be kept one on one. None of our kids dread talking to us after a race. They are always looking for affirmation, encouragement, and ways to improve.

- **Some of the stuff that should never happen:**

  Criticizing a kid in front of team mates,

  Giving a kid the cold shoulder after a bad race, etc.

- **What can you do:**
  Build into the routine an opportunity to talk about what could have gone better, by having the kids write a "review" of their race, not just the bad ones, every one.

If you understand the sport, you know it is all about training, and the actual race is almost an afterthought. That is why realistic goals need to be set. We will discuss performances during a meet especially if they are good! Also we must be straightforward and grounded in reality. For example, one kid was disappointed that she didn't improve as much as some of the other girls. I said, "Lucy, you missed about 20 days of practice for various reasons. I am not saying all those missed practices were not legitimate, but it is not even hard training that gets you good, it is consistent training, and you didn't have that." This same girl was much more dedicated next season and ran much better.

Coaches and athletes must be honest with each other. Whether the athlete wants to run a 6:00 mile or a 1:50 800m, we must be up front and honest. Giving kids unreasonable goals won't help anyone. It will hurt the athlete's confidence, and it will undermine the coach's credibility. Each race is a small step towards a long term goal. Always try for one small step forward at a time.

Photo: Harry Norton at Mayor's Cup. Norton's accomplishments are profiled earlier in the book.
Courtesy photo, Tom Derderian

THOUGHT FOR THE DAY

You can run in the Olympics without ever winning a race.

You cannot run in the Olympics if you don't improve many years in a row.

Photo: Phil Shaw running for Mick Grant's Lynx Elite club at USATF Indoor Nationals, running a 3:06 1200 DMR leg.
Courtesy photo, Jim Rhoades

28. RACE TACTICS

There are many different race tactics to use and we will cover a few of them here. Racing to win is about pacing, positioning, and planning a decisive move.

- The coach and athletes should go over the race goals and plan well in advance of the day of the race. Don't wait until the day of the race or 5 minutes before the race, to come up with a plan. On race day, simply reinforce the plan you came up with a couple days earlier.

- Don't go out too fast. Know what pace you are capable of and run that pace. Younger athletes usually go out too hard, either from lack of experience, lack of pace training, or lack of confidence. This is the single most important race tactic - don't go out too fast! As explained earlier in this section, the coach must provide splits during races and keep athletes on goal pace in races. One of the simplest and most effective strategies that works in almost all race situations is to ignore everyone else and just stay on goal pace for the first 75% of a race, and then in the last 25%, simply race, and try to beat any runners near you.

- Train intelligently and come to the race as well conditioned as possible. Great race tactics can never overcome a poorly conditioned athlete.

- Don't run too far off the rail in the early and middle parts of track races, because you are unnecessarily running extra distance. Late in tight races, it is more important to ensure you are not "boxed" in, than running close to the rail. There will always be a debate regarding the merits of holding a good race position in a pack vs. running extra distance.

- When making a move to pass, pass decisively. This can often discourage your competitors. Don't ever try to inch by competitors; this almost always encourages them to fight you off and you waste precious energy getting by them.

- In general, don't pass runners on turns; pass on straights or coming off turns.

- If it is windy, run behind (draft) other runners for the early and middle parts of the race as an energy saving strategy.

- In cross county races, we should run the downhill sections very fast, do not brake on the downhill, because that wastes energy.

Do not sprint up hills, as this expends huge energy. However, one good strategy is to surge just before the top of the hill as a surprise attack, to give you good momentum going down the hill, and a few extra yards, and this can sometimes psychologically defeat an opponent.

- In muddy or snowy conditions, wear longer spikes for good traction.
- If it is windy, run behind (draft) other runners for the early and middle parts of the race, as an energy saving strategy, and if practicable, pass runners when the wind is with you.
- Late in a race, make only one decisive move and sustain that to the finish. Generally, the weaker our finishing kick tends to be, the further out we need to start our finishing drive. If we have a strong finish, we can wait a little longer. When we commit to a move, we want to "break" our competitor. A superior kicker can wait until the final 100 or 200 to make this move, whereas a weaker finisher must move from 300 to 600 out from the finish.
- Always run hard all the way through the finish line. Don't be the one who gets caught at the tape unexpectedly by easing up just before the line. The only time to consider easing up is when we are in a meet with trial qualification heats, and we are certain to advance to the final.
- When there are qualifying heats and a final, don't save yourself for the final, if it is going to jeopardize your making the final, which is sarcastically called "saving yourself for the final you won't be in". If there is any doubt about whether or not you can make a final, you need to run all out in the trial.
- When there are qualifying heats and a final, don't showboat or run way faster than you need to run to advance to the final; run fast enough so you safely advance.

Occasionally, despite great training and feeling good before a race, we may get into the race and just won't have it on that day. It is important to put our best effort in anyways. If we quit in a race or drop out of a race, it will be easier to quit the next time the going gets tough, and quitting could become a bad habit. The only time a youth runner should drop out of a race is if they are injured.

There are basically two kinds of races;

1. **Trying to win**   These races may not produce a fast time, but learning how to compete to win is a valuable skill.

2. **Trying to run a fast time** These races may not produce a win, but improving is more important than winning. Running at a fast pace, in a pack, is also a crucial skill requiring great focus.

The Molvar Long Term Solution to Improve the High School Competition Structure

Over the last 20 years in club coaching, Mick has seen repeatedly what can happen to kids over the course of a school year. Once kids get to high school, he only sees them during the summer and between seasons. He sees what kind of shape the kids are in when they go off to school, and he sees what kind of shape they are in when they come back from school. After three seasons of racing, few of these young kids have any "money left in the bank". It is easy to see why this unfortunately occurs. Some of these kids have run 50 or more races during one school year. Since we want to send our kids back to school every year in great shape, we spend weeks just letting the kids run easy aerobic miles, in order to get them healthy and excited (recharge the batteries). It is like rehabilitation. The kids have to start building up their aerobic endurance base all over again. If our athlete has no more endurance at the end of the outdoor track season this year than they had at the end of the outdoor track season last year, then that athlete has essentially made little or no long term progress for the year, and that is a shame. Granted, it is expected that endurance will decline somewhat during peak racing, but when kids have gone 9 months without sufficient endurance training, they will have little or no endurance base left at the end of the school year.

We would like to see the school and club system work together to help kids. Some coaches, from both sides, see this as competition for athletes. This makes the situation worse. We need all coaches to work together to help athletes improve. We must look at the big picture, so the athletes have direction and continuity in training. Some school and club coaches already work together to help athletes, but this must be the norm rather than the exception.

The current competition structure is definitely an obstacle in development. Keep in mind that long term development for middle and long distance runners is based primarily on endurance building and also by developing basic speed. Nothing can frustrate the high school coach and athlete more than failing to improve from the previous year. Why does this occur? Heavy lactic acid producing anaerobic repetition work only results in temporary gains. Therefore, if the bulk of the school year is spent on anaerobic training and racing, there is limited long term development of the athlete and some of the improvement that will be seen is simply due to the natural physical maturation process that occurs during the teen years.

The high school competition structure is not the fault of the coaches, and really there is no one to blame. It is a deeply rooted system that has been in place for nearly 100 years and it needs to be changed. I am in no way implying that changing such a deeply rooted system will be easy.

How can we do a better job in developing young athletes for long term success? The kids who will have the best success in college and beyond are usually those who are building a strong aerobic foundation. Additionally, the kids who have the strongest desire to continue with the sport are those who have spent more time on aerobic development. Those kids, who come from heavy interval based programs and over race, sometimes feel "burnt out" mentally, and can hardly wait for their senior year outdoor season to end, and don't compete in college, despite having talent to run at the college level.

I do think that some kids, without the big aerobic foundation, but who work on basic speed, without over racing, can also be successful in college; although, there will be an endurance deficit to make up. A misconception that many people in the sport have is that they think it is a good thing to be aerobically under trained in high school, so that will result in more improvement in college. We have to be careful saying that.

- If kids are **anaerobically** under trained and are not over raced, that is, indeed, a good thing, as they won't be burned out, and they will be hungry for more competition.

anaerobic over training and over racing limits the development of long term potential and can lead to burnout

- If kids are significantly under trained **aerobically** through high school, it is not ideal. I am suggesting gradual, consistent development of aerobic endurance.

kids may give up the sport, since they don't understand the relationship between aerobic endurance training and performance

Aerobic endurance can be increased spectacularly over a long period of time. It is not something you can develop in a few weeks. If young athletes don't develop a solid aerobic foundation in the first few years of training, in college they will be behind others, who have a more developed endurance foundation. Many aerobically under trained high school runners never get a chance to run in college, because they are deemed to be not good enough. Don't delude yourself into thinking it is a good thing to be significantly aerobically under trained in high school. Developing a high level of aerobic conditioning is the most important factor in the long term development of a distance runner.

A scheduling system that allows high school middle distance and distance athletes to train more aerobically and avoid the over racing/over anaerobic training syndrome is important. A form of this is used in some places, but should be the norm. Many of the top middle and distance college programs reformed their similarly flawed system in the 1980s. They eliminated dual meets, reduced the number of competitions their athletes run in, and started their competitive seasons later. In the current, deeply flawed, high school system we have a situation where the good teams get better and the weak teams get worse. This happens because the good teams, with wise coaches, can afford to use early races as high aerobic tempo runs and/or hold out runners, and aerobically train through, and still win these meaningless meets, which keeps the less informed AD's and parents from complaining; so even though their official schedule may call for 15 races, they will only run about 5 all out races. (See **Chapter 21** for a detailed description of how teams do this and you can do this too at your high school.) This affords them a tremendous advantage and allows for more long term development. On the other hand, the weaker teams don't have this luxury and feel pressured to "chase points" and fight tooth and nail to win whatever number of the meaningless dual meets they can win to keep the parents and AD's from complaining, which results in 15 all out races per season, and a team full of fried runners, who make little progress from year to year, other than that which comes from natural physical maturation during the teen years.

Here is my long term proposal for improving the high school competition format:
1. **Eliminate dual meet system and institute a quad meet system**. Instead of 8-10 dual meets, have 3 quad meets. In track, have unseeded heats as necessary, so every kid on the team has a chance to

compete. This allows teams to still face all their traditional league rivals.

2. **Competition schedule should start later, so it can be preceded by a minimum of 4 weeks of training, especially aerobic endurance conditioning, critical for middle and long distance runners.**

3. Eliminate some restrictions on how many events an athlete can compete in. That may sound counter to my above points, but it isn't. It is far better for the runner to double in 3 meets, than to run one race in 10 dual meets. When you are competing in 10 dual meets, you are simply losing too much training time, due to the races, and cutting back on days before and after important races. When we throw in the invitational meets and relay meets, when is there any time left for training?

Fewer meets means:

A. **More training days,** meaning fitter athletes and ultimately better performances. Adding a higher percentage of training devoted to aerobic development and working on basic speed results in better long term improvement. We want a solid month of training consisting primarily of aerobic development and basic speed every season prior to the first competition. WARNING: DO NOT use this time for anaerobic work. Coaches, who have been educated to understand that we first need to build an endurance base prior to anaerobic training, will train their athletes properly, and will enjoy a huge advantage at championship time.

B. Eliminating over racing means athletes will be more hungry for competition and less burned out. It also means less total time in a season spent traveling to and from meets. A huge complaint from the kids is too many days per season are totally wiped out by meets, leaving no time for other activities.

C. Racing should be limited to a maximum of 1 competition per week.

D. Less anaerobic load as a percentage of total training, reducing injury, over training and burnout risk.

E. Larger meets means better competition, better times, more exciting competition, and more interest from parents and fans.

F. Fewer meets means fresher legs for championship time, and faster times.

G. Encourage better relationships between high schools and clubs. Open communication and cooperation will help the development of athletes. Once the egos of coaches are taken off the table, it is easy to see that the only thing that matters is helping young athletes enjoy running and improve. This system should help athletes sustain a positive training environment in between seasons.

MICK'S COMMENTS

I've had the opportunity to speak with both of the two greatest distance runners in history - Haile Gebrselassie and Kenenisa Bekele about what they did for running as kids. They both said that they ran to and from school as children. Haile told me that he ran 10 kilometers each way (6.2 miles each way) and Kenenisa said that he "only" had to run 5 kilometers each way (3.1 miles each way). They also lived at altitude, so they had the advantage of building a huge aerobic base, at altitude, **without any anaerobic interval training and without any races**. They didn't have to worry about running two workouts and two meets every week. Think about it; they put in the miles for years. The aerobic foundation they built is something lacking in most parts of the world. If you want to improve, build a foundation first.

Photo: Some of Mick's Athletes with Haile Gebrselassie. **Courtesy photo, Lynx Elite Athletics/Mick Grant**

E. INJURY PREVENTION

29. SLEEP

"There is no such thing as overtraining,
only under sleeping and under eating."
- Arnold Schwarzenegger

Of course Arnold was talking about bodybuilding and he was exaggerating that there is no such thing as overtraining because there certainly is, but his point is well taken. Never underestimate the positive effect of sound sleep and eating habits, because they allow you to train at a higher level than someone with poor habits, because you will recover and adapt and improve faster. Even if you are doing the exact same training as an equally talented runner, you will improve faster than them, if you have better sleep and eating habits.

Sound sleep habits are critical for your body to recover from the stimulus of the training and then make an adaptive improvement. This is called **Super Compensation**. Super Compensation occurs not when you are actually running, but when you are resting, and especially while sleeping. During sleep, the highest level of hormones are released, so the longer and more high quality sleep one gets, the better resultant Super Compensation. Better sleep habits also reduce the chance of getting colds and other illnesses. The optimum amount of sleep for a child 5-12 years of age is 9-11 hours per night. For teens, it is 9-10 hours and for adults, it is 7-8 hours (see reference below). Due to cultural changes, most Americans now fall well short of these guidelines. Runners in training should make changes in their lifestyles to get in line with these ideal guidelines to get the maximum improvement out of the running they are doing.

Some generally accepted and basic sleep guidelines include:
- ✓ Strive to meet the above recommended hours of sleep.
- ✓ Go to bed and rise at the same time every day; the body thrives on regularity.
- ✓ If you are routinely being awakened by an alarm clock, you are not getting enough sleep and need to go to bed earlier.
- ✓ Dark and quiet are the ideal conditions, so use heavy dark drapes and foam ear plugs as necessary.
- ✓ A cool room about 65 degrees is ideal.
- ✓ Don't exercise too close to bedtime.
- ✓ Don't eat a big meal close to bedtime.

- ✓ Avoid caffeine completely, if possible, and never consume caffeine at night.
- ✓ Re-hydrate soon after your run and earlier in the day, so you don't have to go to the bathroom frequently in the night.
- ✓ Alcohol interrupts proper sleep patterns resulting in poor quality sleep.

Reference National Sleep Foundation "The Biology of Adolescent Sleep" 2009-10-02

30. JOINTS: TAKING CARE OF HIPS, KNEES & ANKLES

Protecting one's joints is critically important. Preventive maintenance goes a long way to ensure keeping the athlete healthy. The three critical joints are hips, knees and ankles. It is pretty hard to run if we have joint trouble. We want to do some "foot rotations" to loosen our ankles, leg swings (front to back and side to side) to loosen hips, and we want to maintain muscle balance in the hamstrings and quads. We want to be sure the patella (knee cap) is tracking properly. When in doubt, always consult a doctor.

Young kids have soft bones and joints. It is very important to plan appropriate practice for kids in order to minimize (or eliminate!) injury risk. Always try to run on soft surfaces to reduce pounding on bones and joints. Treat aches and pains immediately. Growing kids can have growing pains in their knees, so always pay close attention and train accordingly.

Coaches should be sure kids are loosening up joints as part of their regular pre-practice routine.

31. DIET

In addition to staying properly hydrated, you need to eat right when you are training for maximum performance. Keep in mind most of what will follow may be difficult for a student on a cafeteria diet. It is also more expensive to eat right than the typical American junk food diet. It is still important to know what the ideal is and try to strive towards it whenever practical.

The basic guidelines:

1) You need to stay properly hydrated at all times by drinking water. Muscle is approximately 75% water, and even a 1% loss in bodyweight due to dehydration will result in decreased endurance performance and decreased recovery from a run. You can lose up to 1% your weight in water before you are thirsty, so you want to hydrate before you are thirsty. For ideal performance, you want to be fully hydrated before each run. For ideal recovery, you want to be fully re-hydrated as soon as possible after each run. In high heat and humidity climates, you need to be taking in liquids throughout the day. For training runs or races lasting less than 30 minutes, there is no point in hydrating during the run; just ensure you are fully hydrated before the run. For longer runs and especially in hot weather, if you are sweating excessively, you need to drink during the runs. Minimize caffeine intake, especially in hot, humid weather because caffeine causes dehydration.

2) You need to eat a lot of nutritious food. The reason is when you run a lot, you are burning a lot of calories during the run, but more importantly, it raises your resting metabolism, so you burn more calories at rest and when sleeping than sedentary people. You want to have maximum energy for your runs and maximum nourishment to recover from each day's run. Youth runners also are still growing, which also significantly adds to the total calorie requirement. During the base phase, you may want to even gain a few extra pounds as a buffer to ensure you are getting enough energy and nutrients. The reason is you are not racing, so it doesn't matter if you are carrying a few extra pounds; so this ensures you are getting maximum recovery from each run and have maximum energy. Failure to eat enough, especially for women, can result in the dreaded "**Female Triad**" (see below for more info on Female Triad). Male distance runners should never go below 5% body fat, and women should never go below 10% body fat or any level that results in disruption of the normal menstrual cycle. Youth runners should be gradually gaining weight throughout

the year and every year until physical maturity is reached. Only if they have excessive body fat (i.e. greater than 10% for males and greater than 15% for females), should they ever consider losing weight. A coach must carefully monitor this and intervene if a runner is losing excessive bodyweight. This is especially important for females. If the runner continues to lose weight, training must cease completely, and they need to be put under the care of a physician.

3) Not only do you need to eat a lot, but you also need to get a lot of animal source protein. The RDA for sedentary people is only 40-70 grams per day, based on the age and weight of the sedentary person. Experts (see reference below) recommend significantly higher protein intake for endurance athletes. They recommend up to 0.8 grams of protein per pound of bodyweight for an endurance athlete. Therefore, a 70 pound youth runner should get at least 56 grams, a 100 pound runner at least 80 grams, and a 150 pound runner, at least 120 grams. The RDA is designed for sedentary people. Runners have less body fat, than the average person the RDA is designed for. That means you have a higher percentage of muscle (for the same weight average person) and need more protein to maintain that muscle. Furthermore, you are training every day, which stresses the muscles, which requires more protein for repair and to grow stronger. Some protein should be consumed with every meal and especially within 45 minutes of completing a run. Animal source proteins are "**complete proteins**" and contain between 70 and 90% of the essential amino acids, and therefore, are vastly superior to vegetable source proteins, the best of which is soy, which has only 45% of the essential amino acids. Egg whites and red meat are the richest, followed by poultry, fish, and dairy products. These foods are also high in iron, which prevents anemia. Additionally, the iron in animal source proteins is absorbed into the body more easily than vegetable source iron. For all these reasons, vegetarian diets are not common for serious endurance athletes. Higher mileage male runners, and all female middle and distance runners, are especially prone to anemia, so it is essential you get enough iron from these foods. Males running high mileage, and all female runners who only consume the RDA of protein, and get most of it from non-animal sources, are going to be highly susceptible to anemia, and if you get anemia it will set you back months.

Reference: Position of the American Dietetic Association: Nutrition and Athletic Performance, March 2009

4) It is better to eat 5 medium size meals per day, than 2 or 3 big meals. The reasons are multiple. Firstly, your body can only utilize so much protein at one time, about 25-30 grams, so there is no point in eating more than 50 grams (for example, eating more than a ½ pound piece of meat) in one sitting, because the extra protein will not be utilized for muscle repair and maintenance. It is an expensive waste, as proteins are more expensive, and put unnecessary strain on your kidneys. Secondly, your digestive system works more efficiently digesting smaller meals. Thirdly, frequent meals keeps your body continuously nourished with the vitamins, minerals, and nutrients it needs for maximum recovery. Lastly, frequent meals keep your blood sugar levels more stable, so you feel good all day and don't go up and down, which prevents adult diabetes, a growing epidemic in America, caused by sedentary lifestyle, too much sugar, too big of meals, and too high of a percentage of body fat.

5) In addition to animal source protein at every meal, you want to eat some quality carbohydrates at every meal. Quality carbohydrates include whole grains, pasta, fruits, vegetables, and low fat dairy products (which also contain animal source protein), such as skim milk and yogurt. Carbohydrates convert more efficiently into glycogen, which is your main source of fuel as a runner, than protein or fat.

6) You want to minimize processed foods, fatty food, and processed sugar. The reason is these are less efficient fuel sources, generally harder to digest, and in the case of sugar, causes up and down spikes in blood sugar levels, which can result in ugly mood swings. They are also not good for your general health.

One way to do it is eat really well during the week, and limit the junk food treats to the weekends. It is not a good idea to be super strict about minimizing fats and sugar for several reasons.

- ✓ You need some fat in your diet, as it is essential to function normally, and if you go below 15% dietary fat, your body's synthesis of testosterone will decrease dramatically, resulting in poor muscle recovery from training. The ideal is to get 15-20% of your calories from fat.
- ✓ If you deprive yourself completely of junk food treats, you can suffer from cravings, which can lead to other worse problems such as binging.
- ✓ It is often not practical, if you are a student on a cafeteria diet, or if you are in a typical American household.

✓ You will drive your friends and family nuts if you try to be super strict 100% of the time, and the benefits of being super strict versus fairly strict are not worth the extra effort.

If you really want to get into details about ideal carbohydrates, you can focus on carbohydrates that are low on the **glycemic index**. You can look up the index on the internet. Low index (wheat versus white flour, fruits versus sugar, yams versus white potatoes, etc.) are better, longer lasting energy sources, and keep blood sugar levels more stable.

7) The sooner you eat after running the quicker the carbohydrates can replenish your energy (glycogen) stores, and the protein can repair and build the muscles, so you get maximum recovery for the next day's run. Don't delay eating after a run. Before you start the next day's run, you want your body to have a maximum amount of glycogen (energy) stored in the body. Studies have shown the way to get the highest levels of glycogen is to eat carbohydrates immediately after exercise, and eat as much of them as soon as you can. The most receptive time is within 15 to 30 minutes after a run. One way to do this is to down a full glass of orange juice right when you finish running, so you don't have to buy expensive "energy replacement" drinks. Also remember, you need to eat some animal protein as soon as possible (within 45 minutes) to start the muscle tissue repair process. You can also start to satisfy this need by also downing a full glass of skim milk right after a run, which also adds more carbohydrates in addition to the protein. Again, you don't need expensive protein drinks to satisfy this need. An excellent and cheap practice is to get into a habit of drinking orange juice and skim milk right after every run. Even after drinking those, you want to have a full meal shortly afterwards. So never delay eating after running, to ensure maximum recovery before the next day's run, so your progress is accelerated.

8) Ensure you are getting enough calcium in your diet for bone development and growth in youth, and to prevent brittle bones, and the risk of stress fractures. Non-fat milk and yogurt are the best sources and should be consumed generously, provided you are not lactose intolerant. If you are, it is critical that you consume other calcium rich foods and take a calcium supplement. Minimize soft drinks, because they inhibit calcium absorption. Always discuss with your doctor, when taking additional supplements.

9) Take a multi-vitamin every day and vitamin E, which enhances recovery. It is best to meet your body's needs through dietary

food. However, despite your best efforts through eating well, you may not be getting all the vitamins and minerals you need, so take one just in case. Also, women runners need extra iron and should take an iron supplement to avoid anemia. Very high mileage males should also consider taking an iron supplement, but watch out for signs of taking too much, and one warning sign is unexplained headaches. Athletes, who are not consuming generous portions of dairy products, should also consider taking additional calcium. Always discuss with your doctor when taking additional supplements.

10) Pre-Race Meal – The pre race meal should be consumed 2-4 hours before the race. It should be light to medium in size. It should be easily digestible. It should contain a little protein and be rich in carbohydrates. The runner should also be thoroughly hydrated before any race or run. Within those guidelines, each individual runner must discover through experience what works best for them and stick to that. This includes how long before a race, what size meal, and what type of meal. Over time, you will discover your own ideal plan. In rare cases, some runners have to run on an empty stomach, which is a disadvantage, but if that is all that works for them, they have to do that. Here is what works for a lot of runners. Something such as cereal with low or non-fat milk, a banana, and glass of juice is good. We don't want heavy, fatty foods that will sit in the stomach all day. If the competition is in the afternoon, we will need to look at a sandwich or some snacks. We also MUST be sure that our athletes are staying hydrated. Dehydration is common at long competitions. We like our athletes to have both water and a sports drink, such as Gatorade or Powerade. We don't want too much sugar in the stomach, but we do need to keep blood sugar levels to be maintained. For snacks, we like crackers and bananas. **We do not want to see any citrus fruit at competitions.**

11) Sample Typical Day - Here is a sample ideal day. By no means is this the only way; there are many other foods you can substitute following the above guidelines. Also, this is not practicable for most people, and it is also expensive to eat well. I provide it only as a sample, so you have an idea what an ideal might look like that you could strive towards, but not likely achieve. Also, remember to drink plenty of water to keep properly hydrated. When running fairly high mileage, and especially during the summer, you need to be drinking water throughout the whole day.

Meal 1 - Breakfast: 730 AM

3 egg whites with one egg yolk, whole wheat toast or bagel, or no sugar cereal, skim milk, or low fat no sugar yogurt. If you run in morning, drink orange juice first and then skim milk immediately after finishing the run, followed by a meal.

Meal 2 – Mid Morning Snack 1000 AM

½ meat (turkey or tuna with low fat mayo, or roast beef, or chicken, etc.) sandwich, whole wheat bread, skim milk

Meal 3 – Lunch   1230 PM

small piece of fish or tuna, fresh fruit without sugar, skim milk

Meal 4 - Supper 500 PM

meat, chicken or fish, baked potato or pasta, mixed vegetables, bread or bagels, skim milk

If you run before supper, drink orange juice first and then skim milk immediately after you finish the run, followed by a meal.

Meal 5 - Evening snack 800 PM

small piece of leftover mcat, chicken or fish, pasta, skim milk

Warning ! Avoid Female Triad!

The worst thing that can happen to a female runner is failure to eat enough resulting in the dreaded Female Triad. The Female Triad is a combination of disordered eating, lack of menstrual cycle, and fragile bones. If this condition is prolonged, it can result in spontaneous fractures, frequent stress fractures, early onset osteoporosis, and psychological problems with food and weight. If you fail to eat enough total calories or protein or calcium either from simply not paying attention or due to an eating disorder, you are at risk of the Female Triad. Later in the book is an excellent in-depth thesis on the Female Triad by Dr Kristin Cobb. Normally weight training and high impact activities such as running, result in increased bone density, provided there are sufficient calories, protein, and calcium in your diet, and actually reduce the chances of osteoporosis later in life. Runners who have an adequate diet have higher bone density than the general population. So pay attention, eat a lot of total calories, a lot of protein, and a lot of calcium.

We like to tell the kids they are high performance race cars. They are not sticks. Everything about an athlete needs to be ready for high performance, including high performance fuel. I never want the tank empty. Always give athletes positive reinforcement about how fit and fantastic they are. Also make sure that kids know that eating a well balanced diet is crucial not only to endurance training, but to their long term health and wellness. We are looking for healthy, powerful young athletes. Kids are never too young to learn about a healthy well balance diet. We want our kids to be healthy, understand health issues and to have a good self image.

We also like the kids to have a full blood check every year, as part of an annual physical. We want to be sure iron levels are good, so they are not at risk for anemia. The blood test should test for serum ferritin as a minimum, and it is also useful to test for hemoglobin. If serum ferritin is below 40 (and/or hemoglobin below 12), you should begin supplementation following your doctor's orders. If serum ferritin is below 20, you are considered severely anemic. We also want to be sure our athlete has no low grade infections, which is another reason for the blood test.

In summary, coaches and athletes need to understand that the stimulus of the training causes minor damage to the muscular system. If the athlete has sufficient nutrition and rest, the damage is repaired and the muscles grow stronger. The actual improvement takes place when the athlete recovers, through absorbing nutrients from food and resting/sleeping. This subtle point may seem trivial, but if the athlete is not getting sufficient rest, nutrients, and water; they will not recover. You need to eat as soon as practical after a run to facilitate maximum recovery from each workout. You need to include protein for muscle repair, carbohydrates for glycogen replenishment, and water, to replace water lost through sweat.

32. REDUCING INJURY RISK

Following the principles of this book, a runner can increase endurance spectacularly over a long period of time and gradually improve basic speed, regardless of innate talent. To be able to do that, you must be able to train consistently over long periods of time without setbacks, due to injuries and illness. Long time coaches and fans of the sport all over the country are aware of kids, who appeared to have little talent, but trained and trained consistently for many years, and ended up at a ridiculously high level, compared to where they were early in their career, due to their durability and avoidance of injuries. Those same observers are also unfortunately aware of a far greater number of more talented runners, who never went as far in their careers, due to injuries. That is why some people say durability is the ultimate talent in middle and especially distance running.

It should be obvious that a key goal of any developmental program is injury avoidance. This is why Mick's mantra has always been "Have Fun and Stay Healthy". Indeed one of the keys to Mick's incredible success as a youth coach over 20 years was the extremely low injury rate of kids, which allowed them to continue to progress, and as he likes to say, "reveal" their talent. John's sons Joe and Josh started running at ages 6 and 7, and they haven't had a single injury in the 7 years they have been running. Keep in mind that durability, i.e. the ability to train without getting injured, is in itself an innate talent, as some people are simply put together more robustly than others, and it will not be obvious in outward appearance. That said, even the most durable can get injured, and the least durable runner can avoid a lot of problems, so it is important for all runners to follow these guidelines to avoid injury:

1) <u>Don't let little problems become big problems.</u> – The runner must pay close attention to their bodies, and when there is the first hint of something going wrong or hurting, stop running and notify your coach. Don't be afraid of being called a baby. If your coach is experienced in injury assessment and aggressively treating them (i.e. not ignoring them), they can assess if it is a real concern or not, and if not experienced, they can talk to coaches and runners with experience. If necessary, a doctor can be consulted. The key here is don't let a minor problem, which could be taken care of in a couple of days, evolve into a big problem by ignoring it and hampering your training for months.

2) Coaches, pay close attention. – Coaches need to observe the runners, and if they see someone that appears to have some ailment, to stop them immediately. Coaches need to ask their runners after every practice if anything hurts. Even a minor ache, for example, in the achilles or plantar, that the athlete thinks is nothing, can develop into a significant problem with lots of downtime, if it is ignored. Again, the goal is to prevent little things from becoming big things.

3) Treat injuries aggressively. – By aggressively, this means at the first hint of trouble, taking immediate action to stop the athlete from running, get the injury properly assessed, and treat the injury immediately.

4) Start beginners at a very low level. – The most susceptible time to injury is when a beginner first starts training, especially beginner's injuries such as "shin splints" and "Runner's Knee". They have no formal running training before this, so anything they do will be a big increase in stress. Start them off with as little as 5 minutes a day, and slowly increase from there as described in **Chapter 8**.

5) Don't take long layoffs between seasons. – This is the most common mistake coaches make. When you stop running completely after a season, and then you start back up, this is when you are most susceptible to injury. Also, old injuries that you previously overcame can come back when you do this. Not only that, you are needlessly throwing away hard gained fitness from the previous training cycles. Yes, you should cut back and take a couple days off to get mentally fresh and fully recover from the previous season, as outlined in the End of Season Recovery section of **Chapter 7**, but do not stop running completely for 2 weeks or more.

6) Don't over race. – Running all out races puts maximum stress on the body, and therefore, the chance of injury is much higher. Choose races wisely and minimize them as outlined in **Chapter 21**. By simple math, it is obvious your chance of getting injured is lowered by running fewer races. It also reduces the chance of getting illnesses.

7) Minimize anaerobic interval training. – Anaerobic interval training is necessary to race at your best, so your body temporarily gains anaerobic fitness to handle the lactic acid you will encounter in races. However, these gains are not only temporary in comparison to aerobic training as emphasized throughout this book, but this type of training is highly stressful to the body, and hence, the more you do, the higher the injury risk. Limit this type of training to small part(s) of the year as outlined in **Chapter 10**.

8) <u>Always warm-up and cool-down properly.</u> - Far more important than stretching, is warming up properly prior to any run. Any time you do anything fast be it a race, an interval workout, working on basic speed, strides, or tempo runs, warming up is critical to prevent injuries. Even when doing regular distance runs, start slowly for the first few minutes to warm-up. Also a proper cool-down can also prevent injures. Warming-up and cooling-down are outlined in **Chapter 32**.

9) <u>Run with proper form.</u> – Bad form can lead to injury. Follow the guidelines outlined in **Chapter 17** to correct any problems with running form.

10) <u>Pay attention when increasing mileage.</u> – Aerobic distance training is far less stressful than races and anaerobic interval training, and contrary to myth, mileage doesn't cause injuries. However, when increasing mileage, it is safest to do it gradually, and to pay close attention to your body, for any sign of trouble. Follow the guidelines outlined in **Chapter 8**. Don't increase to the next mileage level, unless you have successfully completed the previous level without any problems, and you feel you are ready for the next increase.

11) <u>Always use flying starts for repeats.</u> – Whenever doing any type of repeat, be it sprints, interval training, hill repeats, time trials, strides, etc. always start behind the "starting line" by jogging into and gradually increasing your speed before you hit the starting line. Rapid acceleration from a standing start increases injury risk. Also, never come to an abrupt stop at the end of any repeat.

12) <u>Avoid the use of "crappy" indoor facilities during the winter.</u> – "Crappy" indoor facilities are defined as any unbanked track less than 200 meters in length, or 200 meter tracks that are so crowded with runners and joggers and walkers you have to zigzag your way all over the track, or running in an indoor warehouse, or worst of all, running in school hallways. Running fast in any of these crappy facilities is practically begging for an injury, due to the excessive torques that will be inflicted on your body. You are better off working on your aerobic base and doing any necessary fast running outside on straight flat stretches of road, when they are free of ice and snow, and of course, after a thorough warm-up, and dressed in warm clothing.

13) <u>Get enough sleep.</u> – Getting proper sleep will greatly reduce the chance of illness, and will aid in recovery to muscles and joints, and hence reduce injury risk. Follow the sleep guidelines of **Chapter 17**.

14) <u>Use ice baths.</u> – If you are lucky enough to have the luxury of being able to immerse your lower body in cold water or ice baths, such

as in an ice bath tub or a lake or ocean, right after a run, take advantage of it; it will reduce your chance of injury.

15) Strength training – Strength training will reduce the risk of injury, simply because stronger muscles and tendons are less likely to be injured. Strength training also can improve basic speed, and it is outlined in **Chapter 33**.

16) Be careful with highly pitched roads. – Running on the same side of a crowned road with steep pitches on the side, will result in you running in an unsymmetrical body position and could result in injury. Avoid such roads if practicable, or if you have to use them, alternate sides when safe to do so.

17) Get a blood test at least once a year at your annual physical, and 2 or 3 times a year, if practicable. A full blood check including a test for serum ferritin as a minimum, and also for hemoglobin, if practicable, can let you know in advance if you are heading for an anemic state, which can takes months to recover from if you wait too long. This is especially important for all females and high mileage males. Also request a hard copy of the results, so you can track your serum ferritin and other blood work results, so over time you can find your own personal normal range. If serum ferritin is below 40 (and/or hemoglobin below 12), you should begin supplementation following your doctor's orders. We also want to be sure our athlete has no low grade infections, which is another reason for the blood test.

While the above 17 recommendations will definitely reduce your chance of injury, the following techniques MAY be useful in reducing injury. We say MAY be useful, because these are still widely debated as to their usefulness, and you, the coach, and athlete, must determine the usefulness of these techniques, to your own situation.

17) Choose the right running shoe. – Ah, doesn't that sound great and make perfect sense?!! Of course, but finding the right shoe in the thousands of choices and finding the best one for each runner is a whole industry in itself. Even if you find the perfect shoe for you, it will be replaced by a new model next year and the "improvement" may hurt you. Some say cushioning and stability are critical, while others say the opposite, i.e. minimalism and flexibility are the keys. Our advice is to find the most basic stripped down shoe, without the bells and whistles, that works for you, and stick to that model, and future versions of that model. We don't recommend running barefoot or in rubber glove style shoes. Further complicating the issue is the shoe companies, for obvious reasons, and some "experts", recommend

constantly getting new shoes after some set number of miles. Other "experts" say worn shoes or broken in shoes are less likely to result in injury. Obviously, severely worn shoes should be replaced, because you could be running unevenly. Any further discussion on this topic would rapidly become unproductive.

18) <u>Run on soft surfaces.</u> – Many believe that running on soft surfaces reduces the impact to your joints, and therefore, lessens the chance of injury. Not everyone believes this. Firstly, running on soft surfaces such as trails in the woods and grass fields, usually greatly increases the risk of ankle sprains, which are much less likely on roads. Also, the soft surface may have less impact stresses, but the unevenness of the surfaces can actually put more twisting stresses on the joints. Again, this is an area each individual must find what works the best for them, but the majority of runners at least enjoy trails more, and may also feel they can reduce injury risk, so when in doubt, default to trails, if they are readily available.

19) <u>Stretching</u> – Whatever you believe about stretching, within 3 minutes of searching on the internet, you can find a study backing your particular personal belief. About three quarters of the literature on the subject says that stretching can reduce injury risk, and a small percentage of that literature says it will not only reduce injury risk, but actually improve performance. However, about one quarter of the literature says stretching will not reduce the risk of injury, nor improve performance. Some of these studies say that stretching can actually increase the risk of injury. Still others believe that stretching is only useful in the treatment of injuries, but not injury prevention. Again, you will have to decide what works best for you. If you do decide to stretch, most literature advocates that it be done gently and statically, and is more useful after a run, than before a run.

33.   HOW TO HANDLE INJURY AND ILLNESS

Important: Whenever injury or illness occurs, ALWAYS consult with your doctor and follow their instructions. What follows is informational and is not intended to be medical advice.

Illness

Common Cold: The average American gets 2-3 colds per year. Light to moderate exercise generally improves immunity from illness, but when you progress to more serious training, these factors equalize, and the typical runner will get 2-3 colds a year. If you are getting more than 3 colds a year, something may be wrong; you could be overtraining, or need to change your habits, or may have some medical condition, and you need to consult with a doctor. When you get a head cold, you must back off in your training for the typical 7-14 days a cold lasts. If you keep training full bore, you risk making it worse by spreading it to your chest, or lasting longer, or getting a secondary infection that will set you back even further. When you get a head cold, back off. You can still run easy distance, but cut back mileage, and do no fast running of any kind. If you get a chest cold, you have to back off even further, and consider taking 1-3 days off during the worst of it.

Flu: If you get the flu or have an elevated temperature, you cannot run, and should not do any exercise of any kind, and rest and follow doctor's orders.

Low Iron Anemia: Anemia can strike female runners and higher mileage male runners. We covered in depth how to prevent anemia in the **Chapter 29**. Anemia takes months to come on and months to recover from. That is why we recommend getting complete blood work at least twice a year, and you have to specifically insist that the doctor tests for anemia, because they normally won't test for it with routine blood tests as outlined in **Chapter 30**. Even though anemia takes months to come on, it usually sneaks up on you and you don't realize it, until it is too late. Within a 1-2 week period, you will notice an inexplicable and sudden decline in performance in races and/or tempos. A blood test is warranted, and this may confirm anemia. The blood test should test for serum ferritin as a minimum, and it is also useful to test for hemoglobin. If serum ferritin is below 40 (and/or hemoglobin below 12), you should begin supplementation following your doctor's orders. If serum ferritin is below 20, you are considered severely anemic. It takes several months to recover from anemia. For treatment, you obviously have to increase iron intake following your doctor's order, by eating iron rich foods, such as animal protein, and you have to take an iron supplement. Consume iron with vitamin C (e.g. juice), which helps absorption, but don't consume it with calcium (e.g. dairy products) or caffeine (ex. coffee, tea, or soft drinks that contain caffeine), which inhibit absorption. Some iron supplements can upset your stomach. Some people have said Feosol and Enzymatics Ultimate Iron are easier on their stomachs. The good news is you can continue to run but only easy distance. Not running at all, will not speed your recovery from anemia, so you can run easy, slow distance, but races, tempos, workouts, and anything strenuous, are out of the question for several months, until blood tests reveal your levels have risen back to satisfactory levels. The only silver lining with anemia is that some athletes that continue to do easy distance while recovering, have come back at a much higher level than before they got anemia.

Mono: More than 90% of Americans get exposed to Mononucleosis at some point in their lives, mostly in early childhood, but the illness only has active noticeable symptoms, if it doesn't first strike until the teen years. Teens afflicted with this cannot run or do any exercise for 1 month minimum, up to several months, depending on the severity. Do not attempt to run during the active state, or you will rupture your spleen. Follow your doctor's orders on when you can resume training.

Cross Training

When recovering from an injury, you should do **cross training** to minimize fitness loss. Only do cross training when you can safely do it without affecting the injured area. Since cross training is less effective than actual running, you have to spend more time at it than your normal time running to minimize the fitness loss. The best form of cross training is swimming, if you are a good swimmer and have a pool available. The next best is cycling/stationary bike. If you can't do either, another option is a rowing machine, but it is vastly inferior to the other two.

Injuries

Muscle Strains: Runners can get muscle strains in the quads, hamstrings, calves, and groin area. Based on the severity of the strain, various non-technical generic terms are used such as "slight strain", "slight pull", "strain", "pull", "slight tear", "severe pull", and "severe tear". The higher percentage of the muscle fibers involved, the worst the strain and the longer the recovery time. The treatment is generally the same. The instant you feel even a slight twinge or strain STOP IMMEDIATELY and get down on the ground. Never try to finish your race or rep or whatever you are doing; the sooner you stop, the less damage, and the quicker the recovery. Immediately get ice on the injured muscle. The quicker you get ice on it, the faster the ultimate recovery will be. After you get ice on it, elevate the injured muscle, so it is above your heart. Also wrap the injured muscle and ice to provide compression. All of this is summarized by the RICE principle – Rest, Ice, Compression and Elevation. Do not stretch the injured muscle for the at least the first 48 hours or several days, depending on the severity, or you will make it worse. Stretching immediately after straining a muscle is like pulling on a frayed rope. Do not walk on the injured muscle, unless absolutely necessary. Continue the RICE principle as much as possible, for the first 48 hours. After the initial extended icing, ice for 20 minutes on and 1 hour off. Do not take any anti-inflamatories in the first 48 hours, or you will make it worse. If you have to walk with a severe limp, you should be on crutches, until you can walk with only a slight limp. As soon as you can walk without limping, you should do so, to get blood flow in there to speed healing, and prevent adhesion formation, and then ice after the walk. As soon as you can jog without limping or favoring, you should jog slowly for short jogs, and ice after the jog. After the first 48 hours, you should start using the Stick and Foam Roller gently on the muscle to prevent adhesion formation. Eventually you can start gentle stretching. Fast running should be avoided for at least a couple of weeks after you resume jogging, and it is very important you continue to massage the area with the Stick and foam roller. If adhesions form, they can lead to scar tissue formation resulting in chronic problems with the muscle. Quad injuries generally heal rapidly due to the high blood flow. Hamstring, calf, and groin injuries heal much slower. If you try to come back too soon to full bore training, or fail to massage them, they can become recurring injuries, and you may have to see an Active Release Specialist (ART) to treat the injury. Although outside the scope of this book, frequent calf strains are very common in runners over age 40; use the Stick to massage the calves on a routine basis to prevent recurrence.

Excessive Muscle Soreness: When you have excessive muscle soreness, you need to just do easy distance until is subsides. Taking a day off completely won't help. Massaging with the Stick and Foam Roller may also aid recovery. Don't attempt fast running of any kind. You can tell simple muscle soreness from a muscle strain, because the muscle soreness will be symmetrical, meaning both legs will have soreness, not just one, such as when you have a muscle strain.

Side Stitch: A side stitch is a sharp pain that comes on during a run, and 90% of the time, is just under the lower right rib area, but can also be on the left side, and other areas of your core. There is nothing you can do about it, and they are harmless, and you can and should keep running, but it almost always forces you to slow down; so it is disastrous when you get one in a race. Pressing on it won't help, nor will altering breathing patterns. They can go away during a run but often last the duration of the run. Severe ones can affect two or three runs in a row. The exact cause is still unknown, but the most prevalent theory is it involves "internal pressure in the liver". Generally, the fitter you are, the less likely you are to get them; so beginners and out of shape people, get them more frequently, but even the best runners in the world in top condition can get them. It is believed that running too soon after eating can increase the risk of getting them.

Chaffing: Chaffing can occur almost anywhere on the body, especially between the legs, on the nipples, and under the arms. It usually affects beginning runners more, but running in the rain can cause it, and doing long runs, and especially long races. There are now several stick application sports lubricants that work very well, replacing the messy, staining, and the limited effectiveness of Vaseline and petroleum jellies of the old days. If you get chaffing, use these products, and also use band-aides for your nipples. When doing long runs and especially long races, use the lubricants and band-aides in advance. Severe chaffing between the legs in a long race can get so bad; it can actually knock you out of a race.

Black Toenail: Black Toenail is common in runners who progress to higher mileage. It results in dried blood and swelling under your toenails and on the tips of your toes, and often you get in a cycle where the toenail repeatedly falls off. It is also jokingly called ugly runner's feet and some even see it as a badge of honor, and they say, "The runner with the ugliest toes wins the race." However, it can get so painful that it starts to interrupt your training. The primary fix is, when you are putting on your running shoes, make sure your heel is as far back as possible in the shoe, before you tie them. This prevents the repetitive ramming of the tips of your toes against the front of the shoes.

Blisters: Blisters on the bottom of your feet and toes are a common runner's ailment. To prevent them, you should wear a thin sock as a minimum, wear properly fitting shoes, use stick sports lubricants on problem areas, and start each run with dry socks and dry shoes. Break in new shoes gradually by wearing them every other run or every third run for a couple of weeks to prevent blistering. If you already have blisters, take the above precautions, and use over the counter moleskin or blister pads that protect the area. If the blister is large, and full of clear fluid, and prevents you from running, see a medical specialist who can pop the blister on the edge with a sterile pin, drain the blister, and apply antiseptic to prevent infection. Blood blisters should not be popped. Blisters can get so bad that they can force you to take days off and can get infected, so don't ignore them.

Calluses: Runners can get calluses on their feet and toes when excessive rubbing against the shoe causes the skin to toughen by thickening with dead skin. If they keep growing, they will eventually cause pain in the underlying tissue. When this happens, the treatment is to soak them in warm water, and then use a commercial metal grating shaver to grind the dead skin away. It is best to shave off a little each day for several days, until you get down to fresh skin, than to grind it off all at once. The new commercial metal grating shavers are far superior to the pumice stones and standard files of the old days.

Shin Splints: Shin Splits commonly affect beginning runners and runners who are starting back up after a long break. This is yet another reason to not take complete layoffs after the end of a season. Shin splints are caused by weak muscles in the front shins and tight (calf) muscles in the back. They are characterized by a general pain in the shin area and typically affect both shins, and tend to hurt most at the beginning of a run. There are 5 things you can do.

1) To strengthen the muscles on the front every day, do 2 sets of 1 minute of walking barefoot on your toes, 2 sets walking on your heels,

1 set of walking on the outside of your feet and 1 set of walking on the inside of your feet. Do all of these 3 times/day or as often as you can.

2) To increase flexibility in the back, you need to stretch your calves/achilles. There are online videos showing you how to do it. If you have an incline board, that is even superior to the above stretch.
3) You can ice them after each run for 20 minutes.
4) If necessary, you have to cut back the amount you run, and if they worsen, take occasional days off. The problem with total rest is shins splints come right back after you start up again; so stopping running completely is not advised. Only if they get real bad, take an occasional day off. Also, once your muscles get stronger and the calf/achilles looser, they should gradually go away, but it can take many weeks to go away, so you need to do this routine and be patient.
5) The final last resort thing, is to lean slightly forward when your run, but don't bend at the waist. Often people who have shin trouble tend to run very upright or even lean back slightly and tend to over stride. This puts more pressure on the shins. Don't do a drastic change, just very slight.
Warning: Shin Splints, which are very common among beginning runners and runners starting back up after a lay-off, are sometimes misdiagnosed as "Compartment Syndrome", which is extremely rare and requires surgery. If you are diagnosed with "Compartment Syndrome", get multiple doctor opinions to ensure the diagnosis is correct.

Stress Reaction and Stress Fractures: A stress fracture is a microscopic fracture near the surface of a bone. Runners can get them on the metatarsal bones of the foot, the lower and upper leg bones, and even in the hip bones. The symptom is concentrated pain in one exact spot (as opposed to a generalized pain such as shin splints), and importantly, the pain worsens during the run (as opposed to tendon injuries that feel better after the early stage of the run). They are not visible on X-rays, and therefore, a MRI or bone scan is required to definitively diagnose the injury. If you have concentrated pain, but no visible fracture on MRI or bone scan, then you may have what is called in layman terms a "stress reaction", which could lead to a stress fracture, if you keep running on it. The treatment for a stress reaction is a couple of weeks of no running. The treatment for a stress fracture is 8 weeks of no running, and sometimes a walking boot or cast or even crutches can be prescribed during the first few weeks. Severe stress fractures can take up to 16 weeks of no running. Females are at higher risk than males and the Female Triad athlete, which is described and warned about in **Chapter 29** is at significantly higher risk. Athletes with low calcium intake and/or absorption are also at higher risk. Weight training can also reduce the risk, and is often prescribed as part of rehabilitation, to strengthen the muscles that support the affected bone. As always, follow your doctor's instructions.

Ankle Sprain – An ankle sprain occurs when the ankle is twisted to an extreme, resulting in a partial tear to one of more of the ankle ligaments. In severe cases, the tear can be so extensive or complete that surgery is required. The key to treatment of an ankle sprain is to stop running immediately, and get off your feet. The sooner you do that, the less damage, and the quicker the ultimate recovery. Then you need to get ice on it immediately. The sooner you do that, the quicker the ultimate recovery. You want to elevate the ankle above your heart. You want to wrap the ice and your ankle to compress it to limit swelling. All of this is summarized by the RICE principle – Rest, Ice, Compression and Elevation. In the first 48 hours, you want to continue with RICE, as much as practicable. Do not take any anti-inflamatories in the first 48 hours, or you will make it worse. After the initial extended icing, ice for 20 minutes on and 1 hour off. Keep it elevated as much as possible. Use crutches to get around. Have a doctor evaluate it to determine when you can start running again. For severe sprains a doctor may prescribe a walking boot to allow proper healing. When you return to running, stay away from trails in which you can re-injure the ankle for several weeks.

Runner's Knee: Runner's Knee typically hits beginning runners or runners who have started up again after a lay off, and is caused primarily by the quads being weak relative to the hamstring (back thigh). This causes the knee cap to not track properly in its groove, which causes pain in the front of the knee under and adjacent to the knee cap (patella). The pain is caused by a temporary softening of the articular cartilage that lines the backside of the patella and/or the articular cartilage on the trochlea section of the femur (leg bone) that the patella glides across. The softening will reverse itself and heal, provided you don't try to train thought it. If you train through this for many months, you can do permanent damage to the articular cartilage. This is rare, as usually the pain and/or frustration is too great and the runner stops in time. However, beware of the risk of permanent damage, if you try to train through it for many months.

- ✓ You need to ice to get rid of any inflammation under the patella (which is usually not visible except in severe cases). Just because you can't see any, doesn't mean it is not there, and you need to ice to get rid of inflammation, so it can heal.
- ✓ You have to strengthen the quads, specifically the VMO muscle in the quad, which is the tear drop shaped muscle that attaches at the top inside of the knee. A strong VMO will pull the patella medially (toward the inside) and keep it into the groove.
- ✓ Squats are the by far the best way to strengthen it, followed by leg presses, followed by leg extensions, followed by straight leg raises, followed by quad sets. However, leg extensions tend to hurt too much if you already have "Runner's Knee", so you should NEVER do leg extensions when you have Runner's Knee.
- ✓ First, try squats with no weight. Stand with feet about shoulder width apart, with feet pointed slightly outward. Put your hands on your hips, and squat down until your upper thigh is parallel to the ground. Keep your back as straight as possible. Do 1 set of 10 reps. Do it twice a day. If it hurts, vary your foot position until it feels most comfortable. Every day add a few more reps, until you get up to 50 reps. Gradually, your VMO will get stronger and the knee cap will track better over a few weeks, and the pain will gradually go away. You may have a little pain at first doing the squats. If the pain is really severe, you can't do squats or leg presses; you might have to start out with the "baby" quad exercises, such as quad sets, straight leg raises, then later you can progress to the squats with no weight. The squats strengthen at least 10 times faster than other exercises, so if you can do them without much discomfort, you definitely want to do squats.
- ✓ If pain is too much and changing foot positions doesn't help, you will have to try some of the alternate exercises (leg press or straight leg raises). Some people wait too long to address the problem, and by then the only exercise they can tolerate is straight leg raises and "quad sets". If that is the case, do straight leg raises with foot pointed slightly outward to stress the VMO muscle and quad sets.

✓ There are 3 other things that will help and you should do.

1) Stretch the hamstring. When hamstrings are too tight, they can cause the patella to track laterally (to the outside) and out of the groove. Stretching hamstrings will help.

2) Stretch the IT band and roll the IT band with a foam roller. The IT band partially attaches to the patella, and if too tight, will pull the patella laterally (to the outside) and out of the groove. Stretching the IT will stop that excessive lateral pull.

3) Stretch the patella towards the inside (medially). Sit with both your legs straight on the ground. Place both thumbs on the lateral side (outside) of the patella, one thumb on the top of the outside, and the other thumb, on the bottom of the outside. Push the patella medially (towards the inside) and hold for 5 seconds. Repeat several times. Don't push it laterally (to the outside or it will make it worse).

IT Band Syndrome - IT Band Syndrome is an irritation of the long Fascia that attaches at the hip at the top and runs down the outside of the upper leg, and attaches just below the knee on the outside. It is caused by the band being tight and/or having adhesions or scar tissue in it and the supporting muscles being weak. The pain is almost always felt on the outside of the knee, where the band rubs against the femur bone. "The outside of my knee hurts." The pain can also be felt up higher in the middle of the band, and it is usually a numbing feeling at that location. This injury can put you out for months, if you ignore it. The pain tends to come and go, and usually hits about 1K into a run. It can get worse during the run, or it can stay the same, or it can go away. As the condition worsens, it can hurt all the time, even when just walking. The IT band can also contribute to "Runner's Knee" and Patella Tendonitis (aka "Jumper's Knee") by pulling the knee cap laterally to the outside.

The main treatment is rolling the band with a foam roller, stretching the band, strengthening the supporting muscles, and initially also icing the irritated area.

Rolling – The best thing for IT is using a large foam roller. Videos are available on the internet showing the technique. Use the foam roller and roll the IT Band for 3 minutes a couple times a day to break up any adhesions in the band. You can also use "the stick" but it is not as effective as the large foam roller, but will help. Do not roll the band where it actually hurts, where it slides over the knee bone, or that will make it worse. Start ½" away from that point, and roll the whole rest of the IT band all the way up to the hip.

Stretching – Take 2 minutes 3-4 times a day, including right before and right after each run, to stretch the IT band. Videos are available on the internet showing the technique. The standing stretch is the best.

Strengthening - You need to strengthen the muscle that controls the IT band, the gluteus medius, which is the smaller muscle under the gluteus maximus (your rear end muscle). The gluteus medius helps balance and attaches to the top of the IT band at the hip. You strengthen it by 2 exercises. One is side leg raises. Lay on your side with the injured leg on top. Do sets of 30 reps every day. The other exercise is standing on one leg (the injured leg). Keep the leg fully straight and balance as long as you can, without putting your other leg down, and without holding on to anything, up to 100 seconds. Do this several a couple of times a day.

During the initial phase of the injury, you can ice the area where the pain is, for 20 minutes on, one hour off.

When running, avoid all hills, and run on flat surfaces. Also avoid running on the side of the road, where the road is pitched/cambered at an angle. Run on sidewalks, or wherever you can find that is flat. If you have to run on the side of the road, alternate sides frequently. Also, avoid running very slowly, because the angle of contact results in more rubbing of the band on the femur.

If it starts getting worse, you need to take the occasional day off, but continue to roll, stretch, strengthen and ice it.

Achilles Tendonitis: Achilles Tendonitis (AT) is an inflammation of the thick achilles tendon caused by an overreaction to tiny micro tears in the tendon. Some theorize that there is no actual inflammation, and therefore, they call it tendinosis. Regardless, it typically hurts at the thinnest part of the tendon, but can also be up higher near the lower calf, and can also be rock bottom, where the tendon attaches to the back of the heel. It is a potential show stopper injury (meaning, if not treated, can stop you from running for months), so it cannot be ignored. Usually it comes on gradually, and will get worse if you ignore it. It is usually worst when you first get out of bed in the morning, and then hurts less as you walk around and loosen it up, as the day goes on. It hurts more when you first start a run, then may loosen up during the run. It can get so bad that you can't run at all, and have to walk with a limp. It can get so bad, that visible lumps of scar tissue can be seen on the tendon. It remains, along with Plantar

Fasciitis, the most difficult running injury to treat, because blood flow to the area is very low, so it heals very slowly, especially if it is rock bottom on the achilles.

The primary treatment is some temporary rest from running, icing, and eccentric calf raises. All other treatments have yielded mixed results, as discussed below, and should only be explored, if the primary treatment fails. When you get it, you should take 3 days off from running to allow it to calm down. During this time, you should ice for 10-20 minutes several times a day, with at least 1 hour between icings. On the third day, you should start eccentric calf raises. This exercise is believed to break up adhesions and scar tissue, and is also believed to stimulate replacement of lost collagen in the weakened tendon, and will cure the problem over time. Do the exercise twice per day for 1 or 2 sets of 10-20 repetitions. If you are running, do them before and after each run. Stand on the bottom step of stairs with just your toes on the stairs and holding onto the railings. Use your good calf to raise yourself up (i.e. concentric motion). Then shift all your weight onto your bad leg and slowly lower yourself down (i.e. eccentric motion), resisting the downward motion, but not stopping it. Go as low as possible. Do it barefoot, preferably. There are videos on the internet showing correct execution of the exercise. It may hurt the first few times you do this. If your tendon hurts at the point of attachment, don't go all the way down using stairs, instead do them on the floor. Continue with this exercise and icing until you are completely cured. Start running on the fourth day, but just 1 mile. Do the eccentric calf raises before the run, then do the run, then do the exercise again, then ice. The next day assess how your achilles feels. If it feels the same or slightly better, keep running and gradually increase. If it feels worse, take 2 more days off and continue to do eccentric calf raises and ice. Continue on this system, until you are symptom free and back to full mileage, which could take anywhere from a few days to a few weeks. Do not try any races, tempos, workouts, strides, or sprints, until you are completely symptom free.

Because achilles is so tough to treat, in addition to the primary treatment, there are several other things you can try if the primary treatment fails, and some of these things work for some people, but do not work for others. Regardless of what you try, always consult with a doctor. These include:

Stretching – You can try gentle static stretching, including standing on a slant board which is probably the best method of stretching the lower leg. This has helped some people, but for other people stretching makes it worse, especially any type of dynamic or aggressive stretching.

Heel Lifts – Some people have used over the counter heel lifts, and this has helped some, but for many people, it doesn't work, and you are not correcting the underlying problem.

ART – Active Release Therapy is very helpful for treating many conditions including Plantar Fasciitis, and muscle tears, and has worked for some people, but has not worked for other people.

Strengthening – Strengthening the calves by doing not only the eccentric calves, but the concentric half also (i.e. regular full calf raises), has helped some people with AT, but has made it worse for others.

Long term rest – Some people have beat AT by taking many weeks or even months off. For many people, however, the symptoms return shortly after they return to running.

Changing shoes – If the back heels on your shoes are worn down you should get new shoes or use shoe repair goo to build it up, because this may help solve your AT. If your heels are not worn down, you can also try different model shoes, which can get very expensive, and may not work.

Avoiding Hills – Some people have found avoiding hills helped the problem, but for some people this alone won't work.

Minimalism – Some people have tried the opposite of heel lifts by going with minimalist shoes, or racing flats, or spikes with almost no heels, and running barefoot, or with rubber glove type shoes with success, but this has worsened the condition for other people.

Walking barefoot and using Plantar Nighttime Socks – These methods which are very helpful for Plantar Fasciitis have been tried for AT and worked for some people, but for some people do not help.

Running Hills – Some people have tried just the opposite of avoiding hills by doing hill sprints and it cured their AT, but this probably won't work for most people.

Avoiding heel contact – Some people have placed their feet far forward in the shoe or cut out the back of the shoe so that the achilles never touches the shoe. This can help some people, but for most this will not fix the problem, because it is not the cause of the problem.

Acupuncture – This has worked for a few people, but won't work for most people.

Ultrasound - This has worked for a few people, but won't work for most people.

Surgery – Some people have tried surgery for AT as a last resort with mixed results.

Cortisone shots – We are against getting a cortisone shot for AT. Yes, you will be immediately pain free, but it can weaken the tendon, leading to catastrophic rupture of the tendon several weeks or months later. It is not worth the risk. A ruptured achilles requires surgery, with a full year recovery and difficult comeback, that usually involves overcoming not only AT after the surgery, but PF is also common coming back from the surgery.

Massaging the tendon – Some people have found directly massaging the tendon helps, but others have found it makes it worse.

Massaging the calf – Some people have found massaging the calf by hand or "The Stick" has helped, but for many others it doesn't work.

Plantar Fasciitis: Plantar Fasciitis (PF) is an inflammation of the thick plantar tendon on the bottom of the foot caused by an overreaction to tiny micro tears in the tendon. Typically it hurts at the arch but can often be closer to the heel and occasionally can be closer to the big toe. It is a potential show stopper injury (meaning if not treated can stop you from running for months), so it cannot be ignored. Usually it comes on gradually and will get worse if you ignore it. It is usually worst when you first get out of bed in the morning, and then hurts less as you walk around and loosen it up, as the day goes on. It hurts more when you first start a run, then may loosen up during the run. Along with achilles tendonitis, it is the most difficult running injury to treat, which is why so many treatment options are offered.

The initial treatment is rest, icing, stretching and massaging it. You can do all 3 in one by filling a round plastic water bottle with water and freezing it. After your run, roll your foot over the frozen bottle back and forth the full length of the foot and press down as you roll. Do this for 20 minutes. This ices it, which reduces inflammation. Pressing down on it, stretches the tendon, so it becomes longer, so there is less tightness on the tendon. The rolling back and forth massages it and breaks up any adhesions and minor scar tissue that may have developed. After icing for 20 minutes, wait an hour, then do it again for another 20 minutes. Do this as often as practicable throughout the day. You should also use "the Stick" to massage it several times a day. Some people have also successfully used a golf ball to massage it. Also, whenever possible during the day, walk without wearing shoes, which will also help loosen the tendon. Because this is a potential show stopper injury, you have to assess how it feels every day. If it feels worse than it did the day before, you have to take off from running and continue treatment. If it feels the better or the same, continue treatment and you can keep running but only easy distance. Races, interval training, sprints, and tempos are out of the question, until you heal completely. You should also reduce the length of your normal runs.

If it fails to respond to the icing, stretching, and massage, the next step is to continue doing these, but also buy "The PF Sock" from a drug store or online which is a special sock you wear at night while sleeping. The sock keeps it in a stretched out position, so it cannot tighten up overnight. Overnight, it usually tightens up a lot, which is why it hurts so much first thing in the morning.

If this fails, the next step is to see a specialist who specializes in Active Release Therapy (ART). A regular doctor and most "sports medicine doctors" usually don't offer this treatment. We are against getting a cortisone shot, as it will weaken the tendon and could cause it to rupture.

Some people have successfully treated PF with orthotics, but this does not work for many people.

Some people have used taping methods to treat PF, but this does not work for many people.

An absolute last resort, and this would only apply to someone who has had chronic PF for a long time, is to get surgery to remove the scar tissue that is so significant and so mature that massage and ART can't release/break it up. Some people have had success with this surgery and others haven't, so it is an absolute last resort.

Hip Tendonitis – Hip tendonitis can creep in slowly over time, and you cannot ignore it, or it will put you out for many weeks. The treatment is icing, massaging, and strengthening. Ice right after a run for 20 minutes. Ice additional times for 20 minutes with 1 hour between icings. Massage the entire area around the hip with a foam roller, using your body weight. This includes the quads, the IT band, and the outer hamstring. Also massage the soft tissue above the hip bone on your waist with the foam roller. Strengthen the supporting muscles by doing side leg raises with the injured leg both ways – with the injured leg on top and with the injured leg on the bottom. Do 1 set of 20 reps a day. Also, do a lateral movement exercise such as shuffling sideways back and forth, while always facing forwards, within a 10 yard area, for about 1 minute. Also, stand on one leg (the injured leg), as long as you can or up to 100 seconds.

Sciatica – Sciatica is pain radiating into your leg due to a lower back injury. The most common location is the glute and/or hamstring but it can also be in the calf and rarely in the outer foot, groin or quad muscles. The pain can be intermittent or constant, mild, or severe. It can be sharp or numbing, and can also result in partial loss of control of the affected muscle, resulting in clumsy motion. It may or may not be accompanied by pain in the lower back, where the problem exists. It can range from completely debilitating, where you can barely move without severe pain, to a minor annoyance you feel on some runs, to anything in between. Sciatica is caused by a fissure or rupture in one of the lower back discs, and the debris material inside the disc leaks out and presses against a nerve. It rarely affects anyone under age 16, because the disc material is flexible and unlikely to rupture, but discs hardens with age and affect people with the highest concentration in the 35-45 age group. Which nerve it impinges against will determine which leg muscle is affected. If the disc material misses hitting any nerve, you won't get sciatica and may only notice a sore back for a few days. The sciatica goes away when the disc material gradually dissolves, and is no longer pressing against the nerve. This can take a few days or up to one year. Surgery is not recommend until after one year, because they have discovered at the one year point the people who didn't have surgery were just as well off, as the people who did have surgery. About 90% of people are symptom free by 1 year. So the primary treatment is rest and anti-inflammatories and icing the lower back for the first couple of weeks. After that, time is the cure. You can run, if and when you reach the point you can run, without favoring anything, or running awkwardly (which can cause another problem elsewhere), and when the pain is tolerable.

Hamstring Tendonitis – Hamstring tendonitis occurs when one of the two hamstring tendons in the back of the knee become inflamed; usually the outside one has the problem. The treatment is icing the tendon and using the stick and foam rollers to massage the hamstring. Directly massaging the tendon itself may work. It is necessary to take days off from running any time the conditions worsens.

Patella Tendonitis/Jumper's Knee: Patella Tendonitis, which is also called "Jumper's Knee", can also affect runners who never jump, but is rare. It is characterized by pain due to inflammation in the patella tendon, which attaches the patella (kneecap) to the lower leg bone. In most cases, the pain is right at the point of attachment of the tendon to the bottom of the kneecap. It also can hurt in other parts of the tendon. It can hurt when running, but hurts the most when squatting or going up stairs. As it worsens, it can start hurting going downstairs, and even just walking. Usually you can't see any visible swelling. Sometime symptoms are erratic, and it can appear to be gone, then suddenly come back with a vengeance.

The causes can be multiple, but the most common cause is tightness in the tendon itself, due to adhesions, or scar tissue building up in the tendon. Weak quads, specifically the VMO (the tear drop shaped muscle on the inner thigh just above the knee), can cause the patella to track incorrectly, putting stress on the patella tendon. Tight quads and tight hamstrings can also contribute to the problem. The IT band also attaches to the patella and if it is tight, it can pull the patella laterally to the outside and cause stress on the patella tendon.

The primary treatment for patella tendonitis is eccentric one legged squats on a decline board. You stand on a decline board of about 20-40 degree pitch facing the downhill direction with one leg (the bad leg). You very slowly squat down to a "half squat" position (i.e. until your upper and lower legs form a 90 degree angle), then raise yourself back up with your good leg. So you do the eccentric part of the movement with your bad leg and the concentric part with your good leg. There are videos on the internet showing the exercise. Only go down with the bad leg and come back up by using the good leg. Have chairs or tables or counters or railings close by to gently touch for balance, as necessary.

Before you start the eccentric squats, you must first stop running for several days and ice for 15 minutes several times a day, until the knee calms down, and is out of the acute inflammatory stage. Then you start the eccentric squats, and always ice for 15 minutes afterward, and several more times, with an hour between icings.

You will likely find you are extremely weak and shaky on this exercise, which is why you have the problem in the first place. Do it twice a day, morning and evening. Start with 10 reps, and over a few days build up to 15 reps, then 20 reps. Start out going slightly down, until you gain some strength, and eventually get to the half squat position.

Initially, you will likely feel some pain. As long as the pain does not worsen, continue to do them. Any time you notice the pain worsening, back off and take a day off from them. You can start running very short easy distance, once you can walk and go up and down stairs pain free. This may occur within one week or may take many weeks. Start with short easy runs. Races, interval training, tempos, and strides are out of the question, until you are sure you are out of the woods. This is a fairly difficult to treat injury, and it may come back again, and you may have to start, stop, and start up running again a few times, before beating it for good.

There are also several other things you can try in addition to the primary treatment. Keep in mind these other things have a mixed record at treating this difficult condition:

Massage - Directly massage the tendon. This can be done with your thumb, or a golf ball, or an elbow, or some other small hard object, or even "the stick". You need to aggressively massage it for 5 full minutes a day, and you need to do "cross friction" massage, meaning not just up and down the tendon, but across it, and you should emphasize the top of the tendon, where it attaches to the knee cap. This works for some people, but for others does nothing, and for some people actually makes it worse.

Stretching - Stretch the quads and hamstrings and the IT band. If the IT band is very tight, you may need to stretch it and massage it with a foam roller. These alone won't cure the condition, but may help a little.

Other strengthening exercises - You can also strengthen the VMO quad muscle by doing the baby quad exercises, which are "quad sets" and straight leg raises with the foot pointed slightly outward. Leg extensions, leg presses, and regular squats are out of the question, until you are completely symptom free.

Long Term rest – Doing nothing for an extended time has cured a few people, but usually fails, as the condition comes right back, as soon as they try to run again.

Also, only go for patella tendon surgery as a last resort, as the success rate is mixed, and can result in worse complications.

Medial Knee Pain – Medial knee pain, i.e. pain on inner side of the knee at the joint between the upper and lower leg bones, is usually a more serious injury that requires immediate consultation with a doctor.

34. WARM-UP & COOL-DOWN AND STRETCHING & FLEXIBILITY

A) Warm-up

It is very important to warm-up prior to each hard workout or race to reduce the chance of injury and to improve performance. You only need to warm-up for 10-20 minutes easy, followed by 2 to 4 "pick-ups" or what some people call "strides" or "striders". For pick-ups, run about 100 meters, and gradually increase the speed, so the last couple pick-ups are equal to or slightly faster than the anticipated pace in the race or workout. For a XC race or tempo, these will not be very fast, but for a 400 or 800 race, they will be very fast. With experience, you will determine which end of the warm-up range (10-20 minutes), and number of striders, that work best for you. Catch your breath, then do very light jogging near the starting line, to keep your heart rate elevated, and your muscles warm, until the gun goes off. Don't waste energy jumping up and down, unless you are a sprinter and will be using blocks. Stay relaxed and review your race plan or workout plan in your head, and don't worry what anyone else is doing. The warm-up serves two purposes. It warms the muscles, making them more supple, which reduces injury risk, plus it raises heart rate, so that your system is not jolted when the race starts. If you fail to warm up properly, you will feel lousy for the first part of the race or workout, until your heart rate goes from resting to race pace. In the olden days, they used to call this "getting your second wind". You can't afford to have this happen in a race. You need to be in your "second wind" before the race starts. This is because when you first start running, your anaerobic system starts instantaneously, but it takes a couple of minutes before your aerobic system kicks in and takes over. A mistake many runners make is to warm up an hour or more before the gun goes off, then lay down, and their heart rate goes back to resting, and the warm up was a waste of effort and energy. By the time the race starts, they are no longer warmed up. You don't have to start a warm-up more than 35 minutes before the gun goes off. If you do, you are warming up too much and wasting energy, or you are allowing yourself to cool down before the race starts, which defeats the purpose of the warm-up.

You should also "warm-up" before normal distance runs by running the first few minutes easy, before you gradually speed up into your normal training run pace.

B)   Cool-down

After a race, or an interval workout or tempo run do an easy cool-down jog. The cool-down run should be at an easy pace, and it is not necessary to do more than 10-20 minutes, unless you are trying to get in extra mileage in for the day. The purpose of the cool-down is to get circulation increased again, which will speed the removal of the lactic acid waste products produced from the anaerobic effort, resulting in a quicker recovery, and less soreness the next day. You want muscle fibers to cool down while still long. Do not blow off the cool-down, or wait too long after the race or interval workout to do it, or you will have excessive soreness the next day and slow your recovery.

C)   Stretching and Flexibility

This aspect of training is important but frequently neglected. How fast we run is determined by the stride rate multiplied by the stride length. It is important to maintain and develop flexibility so we have full range of motion and optimal stride length. Ignoring stretching and flexibility will result in muscle shortening and stiffness and, as a result, reduced stride length. A good stretching and flexibility routine for kids might only take 10-15 minutes and can cover all muscle groups and joints. We want to work on achilles, calves, hamstrings, quads, back, abs, arms, and shoulders. Never do hard, aggressive stretching. This can lead to injury. Jog easy, and stretch easy, to begin and end, every workout.

Photo: Keara Thomas winning open 5k at Boston's Mayor's Cup
Courtesy photo,
Victah Sailer/photorun.net

35. SUPPLEMENTAL CORE AND WEIGHT TRAINING

1)   Core Training

The core is a central meeting point of major muscle groups. The core includes the upper and lower abdominals, obliques and intercostals muscles in the middle of the body. We want a strong core, in order to maintain proper running posture, and maximize the strength of these muscles to aid breathing. Once core muscles fatigue, our athletes will have difficulty in running tall. If our athlete begins to lean forward when they begin to tire, it will make their form less efficient. Additionally, their breathing will be impacted, because their intercostals can't fully expand and contract with each breath. Less oxygen in will increase oxygen debt, and we get into trouble in a race. Leaning forward will also impact stride length, because knee lift will be affected. Core strength is very important. **Youth teams practice should not last too long, so we recommend teaching the fundamental importance of developing core strength over time, but just work a couple basic exercises.** As the athlete gets older, more attention can be paid to core strength. We recommend crunches to strengthen the abdominals, about 3-4 days a week. A good core exercise program will include twists, to strengthen the obliques and intercostals, and should be incorporated into the stretching and flexibility portion of practice. Our stretching routine also includes balancing, which works on core stabilizers. Any stretch which is performed on one leg, like quad stretches, works core muscles a little. We mainly want to teach our young kids about the importance of developing a stronger core each year and how core strength affects running.

2)   Weight Training

Warning: Never attempt weight training without first getting clearance from your doctor. Never attempt weight training without being supervised by a trained expert.

Weight training is a controversial subject for middle and distance runners. There are well respected coaches who say it is useless (Lydiard), there are well respected coaches (Cerruty, Coe, etc.) who say it is essential to reach your full potential, and every opinion in between. We won't attempt to solve this debate here, but will offer a few points.

Why Lift Weights?

While running is the most important training for the competitive middle and distance runner, weight training is a supplement to your running, and can provide the following benefits:

- decreases the chance of injury for runners and other athletes and in daily tasks
- improves one's basic speed
- builds bone density, which will reduce the chance of fracture and stress fractures
- ensures that all your muscles are exercised and strengthened, resulting in a balanced physique

Caution: Lifting weights becomes detrimental if you gain too much weight, because the improvement you get from increased basic speed will be cancelled out by your weight gain. You have to find the ideal balance for optimum race performance. If you gain too much muscle, simply discontinue weights for a while, until you atrophy back to an ideal size. Normally this is not a problem for most females and males under age 16, who are doing a significant volume of running. However, males over 16, who are doing a low or medium volume of running, need to be aware of this risk and curtail weight training as necessary.

What Age Can You Start Weight Training?

Youth runners should not do any weight training, until they reach puberty. Prior to puberty, they should focus on core work, as described above, and do basic freehand exercises 2-3 times per week of 1 set of push-ups and chin-ups.

Once a youth runner reaches puberty, they can begin supplemental weight training, but must meet 3 conditions:

1) Clearance from their doctor

2) They must be under direct supervision of an expert trainer 100% of the time, until they reach age 16.

3) They must only be allowed to use "**Light Weights**" until age 16. Light Weights are defined as weights that are light enough, such that they can get at least 12 reps. They should never use "**Heavy Weights**", which are defined as weights that are heavy enough, so you can only get 4 or less reps.

If the above conditions cannot be followed, put off weight training until age 16, and stick to the freehand exercises of crunches, push-ups, and chin-ups. Unsupervised early teens, who don't know what they are doing, or who are doing stupid stuff like one rep max lifts, or using sloppy form, or fooling around in the gym, put themselves at risk of injury, and should not be lifting weights.

How to get the most out of weight training in the shortest amount of time?

Remember the best thing for running is running, so that must be your primary focus, and any supplemental weight training you do, needs to be a small part of your time and energy. An advantage of a 10 minute workout, is you will never burn out mentally; whereas, if you are facing a 1 to 2 hour workout, you will always have a million excuses not to do it. You can literally do it the rest of your life, without ever burning out mentally.

When to workout?

You can do it anytime during the day, but it is less effective right after a run, as you are too drained to get an intense workout in. It is best to do it immediately before you run, or a few hours before you run. At first, you will find running right afterwards tough, but you will get used to it after a few weeks. Also, you will feel it for the first 2 miles of a run, but then you will feel better after 2 miles. Discontinue weight training the last couple of weeks leading up to the championship part of your season, because you want all your energy going into recovery.

The Routine:

Warning: Never workout without a buddy to help you out, and if you are under age 16, never workout without direct supervision 100% of the time by an expert.

The weight routine is designed to get the maximum possible gains in a 10 minute per day workout. It uses the best possible exercises, in the best possible order, with the optimum daily schedule. Any deviations from it, will result in slower progress for most people. You can modify it to suit the equipment you have available and your schedule, but I would keep the day/muscle rotation as close as possible to the schedule. The routine also varies the rep range from high, to medium, to low, and then repeats the cycle. High reps increase muscular stamina, low reps increase strength and explosiveness to increase your basic speed, and medium reps add muscle size. You want to incorporate all three into your routine. Also, constantly changing the reps shocks the muscle, so you improve faster.

Warning: As stated above, until you reach age 16, you can only use "light weights", which are weights that you can get at least 12 reps. This also applies to anyone over age 16, who is just starting out; they should stick to "light weights" for a few months, until they master proper form.

You will get the quickest results using mostly free weights. If you don't want to use free weights, I have included a freehand exercise program at the end, which hits all the muscles without using weights. Progress is slower if you use machines at a gym, or some other gimmicky contraption you saw on TV, etc., instead of free weights, and even slower, if you use freehand exercises, but they all are better than nothing.

Commercial gyms are fine, but if you really want to save time and money over the long run, I would invest the money to buy equipment for your home. You can use it the rest of your life and buying the equipment will pay for itself in less than a year, compared to joining a gym and paying monthly fees. Also, going to and from a gym wastes time, and you have to wait to use equipment, and the hours are not always convenient.

Take a timed 2 minute rest between each set. You can go on the Internet to see videos by experts on how to do the exercises with proper form:

Day 1
Primary: Biceps & forearms
Barbell Curl: 1 set
Reverse Curls with barbell 1 set
Wrist Curls with barbell 1 set

Day 2
Primary: Chest & shoulders, Secondary: Triceps
Bench Press 1 set
Incline Bench Press 1 set
Dips (leaning forward to focus on chest) 1 set
Lateral Raises with dumbbells 1 set
Bent Over Lateral Raises with dumbbells 1 set

Day 3
Primary: Legs
Squats 1 set
Lying Leg Curls 1 set
Standing Calf Raises (If you don't have a machine, use leg press machine to do "toe presses", or do one legged calf raises on stairs.) 1 set
Seated Calf Raises 1 set

Day 4
Primary: Back Secondary: Biceps, forearms
Chin-ups (Use shoulder width grip with palms facing towards you.) 1 set

Bent Over Barbell Rowing 1 set
Day 5
Primary: Triceps Secondary: Chest, shoulders
Close Grip Bench Press with E-Z bar (preferred) or straight bar 1 set
Lying Triceps Extensions with E-Z bar (preferred) or straight bar 1 set
Cable Pushdowns 1 set
Dips (upright to focus on triceps) 1 set
Day 6
Rest
Then repeat cycle. It is a 6 day cycle, not a 7 day cycle. Also do
1 set of crunches and 1 set of twists every other day or so for core.
Don't do them every day.

Intensity is the key to this program, not volume.
The first time you do it, select a weight that you can get 20 reps in
before **failure**. The next workout, 6 days later for that same exercise,
slightly increase the weight. Every workout, increase the weight, until
you can only get about 3 reps. (**If you are a beginner, or under age
16, don't go below 12 reps).** Then the next workout, lower the weight
to a weight that you can get 20 reps in, and repeat the whole process.
This rotation shocks the muscle, so it can never get used to the same
weight or high reps vs. medium reps vs. low rep, so progress is
accelerated. Also, you get strength and explosiveness for speed from
the low reps/heavy weight, and muscular endurance from the high
reps/light weight, and some muscle size from medium reps/medium
weight.
Example:
For bench press say you can get 20 rep for 50 pounds. So the first
workout, you do 50 pounds and do one set and get about 20 reps. The
next workout, 6 days later, use 55. The next workout,
use 60 and so on. Eventually, at say 100 pounds, you could only get 3
reps. (**If you are a beginner, or under age 16, don't go below 12
reps**). The next workout, drop down to a weight that you can get about
20 reps, which might now be 55 pounds, and start the process all over
again.
The advantage of this workout, is it only takes 10 minutes a day, but in
those 10 minutes you will get the most possible gains you can get. You
don't want to devote more than 10 minutes a day to weights, if you are
trying to run a lot, along with other daily commitments.
If you don't want to use actual weights, you will get less out of it (i.e. it
will take longer to get the same results), but here is what to do. It is the

exact routine as above, but with no weights:

Day 1
Chin ups: (arms shoulder width apart and palms facing towards you) 1 set to failure
Day 2
Push-ups: 1 set to failure
Push-ups with legs elevated on chair or bed, 1 Set to failure
Dips: 1 set to failure
Day 3
Squats with no weight - keep back upright, go all the way down 3 sets of 25
Standing calf raises on stairs- Keep knees straight hold onto post for balance and do one leg at a time. 1 set to failure each leg
Day 4
Chin-ups (arms shoulder width apart and palms facing towards you) 1 set to failure
Day 5
Hands close push-ups with hands 3 inches apart, 1set to failure
Day 6 rest
Then repeat day 1

Do one set of crunches and twists every other day or so. Don't do them every day.

36. DRESSING FOR THE ELEMENTS

Common sense is the overriding guide when it comes to dressing for training and racing. In general, you want to be comfortable and lightweight, but here are some rough temperature guidelines. These guidelines do not factor in wind and humidity, which you need to factor in.

Training dress

Above 70 degrees Fahrenheit: Shorts and tank top or shirtless for boys.

55-70: T-shirt and shorts

45-55: Long sleeve shirt and shorts

Below 45: Add warm-ups or tights, top and bottom, and light pair of gloves. Note that many runners don't wear gloves, when it is below 45, but if you don't want your hands looking like the hands of a 70 year old when you are only 40 years old, wear gloves.

Below 20: Add hat and heavy pair of gloves

Below 5: Need ski mask hat and extra layers of warm-ups

If running in strong sun exposure, use sunglasses, and sunscreen, and a light, white hat with visor to protect you from the harmful rays. There have been athletes training in the extreme sun of the South and Southwest, who have gotten skin cancer prior to age 50.

When running in cold rain, it is nice to wear waterproof gear, if you can afford it.

It is also good to have a back–up pair of training shoes to wear in the rain. Also, use a sports lubricant to prevent chaffing.

Race dress

Above 45: Wear shorts and tank top/racing singlet.

Below 45: Wear long sleeve shirt under your tank top/racing singlet and light pair of gloves.

Below 35: Wear tights to cover your legs.

Below 20: Wear hat and heavy pair of gloves

Any time it is cold, make sure you are thoroughly warmed up (**see Chapter 32**), and keep your warm-ups on until the last possible minute, before the gun goes off.

Any time it is warm weather before a race, dress lightly, stay out of the sun, and be in a cool place, if possible, until you are ready to warm-up, and of course be properly hydrated.

For track races, spikes give you about a ¼ of a second per 400 meter lap advantage over flats. At the early youth and lower youth level, this advantage is meaningless, so spikes are not necessary. Also remember the Hershey Meets prohibit the use of spikes. As you move to a higher level, you need spikes, so you aren't at an unnecessary disadvantage. If you do use spikes, be sure you wear them in practice several times before you use them in a race to break them in and make sure your feet are used to them, so you don't get blisters. Although outside the scope of this book, since youth runners should never be racing at longer than 5000 meters, wearing spikes in practice frequently prior to a 10000 meter race on the track is critically important, otherwise blisters and/or the resulting calf soreness will be debilitating and hamper training for up to a week.

For cross country races, long spikes give you an advantage if the terrain allows you to wear them. This advantage increases in rainy and muddy weather, and becomes a huge advantage in late season snow races. Regardless, early and lower level youth don't need to worry about spikes, until they reach a higher level.

Ideal Race Temperature
Although you can't control the weather, and you need to be ready to compete in all conditions, one should be aware of the ideal conditions which are listed below. Also keep in mind, many spectacular performances and even world records have been set outside of these conditions.

100/200/400 75 degrees Fahrenheit or higher
800 65-75 degrees
mile/1500 60-70 degrees
2 mile/3000/steeple 55-65 degrees
5000 50-60 degrees
10000 48-58 degrees
marathon 45-55 degrees
Heat Acclimation
If you are going to be racing in high heat and/or humidity conditions, it takes 2 weeks of training in those conditions to become acclimated. If

you go into a high heat and/or humidity without prior acclimation, your performance relative to acclimated runners will severely suffer. Also, remember that high heat in long races can be dangerous even for a highly conditioned runner with no medical conditions.

Altitude Acclimation

If you are going to be racing at altitude (greater than 1000 meters or 3300 feet above sea level), it takes 6 weeks of training at altitude to become acclimated. If you go into an altitude race longer than 800 meters without prior acclimation, your performance relative to acclimated runners will severely suffer, and the longer the race, the more your performance will suffer. If you are attempting to get altitude acclimation, it is important that you only do short easy runs and striders for the first 10 days, to ease into it. If you dive right into it, you will never recover from the first week, and your trip to altitude will be a disaster.

Benefits of Altitude Training

- It is widely accepted that all else being equal, athletes who have ancestors who have evolved at altitude have a slight genetic edge, but they can still be beaten with superior training.
- It is widely accepted that athletes who train at altitude, will have a huge advantage in races at altitude versus athletes who train at sea level.
- The benefits of training at altitude for a sea level race, are still hotly debated. There are some who say it is essential to reach your full potential. There are others who say it offers no advantage. There are others who say the benefits cancel out the drawbacks. There are others who say the ideal is to train at sea level, and live at altitude, or sleep in an altitude tent i.e. "live high, train low". There are others who say it is an advantage to do your base phase at altitude, and a disadvantage to do you anaerobic phase at altitude. The debate will continue, and if you reach a high enough level in the sport, you will have to find out what works best for you.

37. FEMALE ATHLETE TRIAD

THE THIN LINE BETWEEN HEALTHY AND AT-RISK YOUNG RUNNERS

Advice for Preventing the "Female Athlete Triad" Interview of Kristin Cobb, PhD; previously published at kidsrunning.com, youthrunner.com

From Dr. Cobb:
"Please remind your readers that the majority of children in this country are much more at risk for obesity these days than for eating disorders. Children who exercise and run regularly are reducing their risk for many chronic diseases in later life, so these behaviors are to be encouraged; as long as parents and coaches watch out for the signs of eating disorders, catch them early, and explain the severe consequences to girls who are starting these behaviors, I do believe that these problems are extremely preventable."

Mick: Dr. Cobb, We have heard more and more reports recently about the importance of female runners keeping a healthy lifestyle.
Dr. Cobb: Running can be the cornerstone of a healthy lifestyle for your child, as it prevents depression, promotes confidence and self-esteem, and wards off many chronic diseases. However, girls who run are at risk for a serious disorder known as the "female athlete triad", which is a combination of disordered eating, lack of menstrual periods, and fragile bones. This syndrome may lead to early osteoporosis and spontaneous fractures, prolonged psychological difficulties with weight and food, and anorexia nervosa and bulimia nervosa. The good news is that eating disorders and associated problems can be prevented, if young girls are educated about proper nutrition and encouraged to run in moderation.

Mick: What is osteoporosis and what causes it?
Dr. Cobb: Though we think of osteoporosis as an old person's disease, it is a disease that takes root in the young. Estrogen and nutrition are critical factors in a girl's bone development, and if they are not sufficient when a child is young, her bones will suffer in later life. The critical time for building the skeleton is in the early teenage years, just before and after puberty. Peak bone mass is achieved by a woman's late twenties. After this, she loses a little bone each year. Therefore, if a young girl fails to build sufficient bone in youth, she will develop

thin bones (osteoporosis) much earlier in life than a woman with a healthy bone reserve.

Young women runners, who want to be lean for their sport, often restrict the amount or types of food that they eat. Meanwhile, they are burning hundreds of calories through exercise. The resulting energy drain may lead to menstrual disturbances - in trying to conserve energy, the body decreases its production of estrogen and prevents menstruation. Without sufficient estrogen and nutrition, bone development slows and bone loss may even occur.

If a girl is undernourished during the critical time when she's supposed to be building bone, these years of deprivation will be written into her skeleton, much like narrow tree rings reveal a history of drought. Though some recovery is possible, the damage can never be completely erased.

The longer disordered eating behaviors and menstrual irregularities persist, the greater the detriment to the skeleton. Some women runners in their twenties and thirties have bone strengths that would be normal for a 70-or 80-year old women. They may spontaneously break an arm, rib, leg, hip, or vertebra. Additionally, their chance for developing a stress fracture is high.

Mick: What are the most important components of a high performance diet? What MUST a female athlete be sure to eat and drink every day?
Dr. Cobb: There is no one "magic" food that will guarantee high performance. Most importantly, young female athletes should be discouraged from restricting their diets or becoming too rigid in their food choices. Female athletes must eat enough calories every day to sustain their energy output; the calories should come from a well-balanced, varied diet that includes not only fruits and vegetables (the foods we typically think of as "healthy"), but also sufficient fat and protein. Growing girls also need to get at least 1200-1500 mg. of calcium every day. This is most easily obtained from eating 3-5 servings of dairy products, such as yogurt, milk, and cheese. Other calcium-rich foods include leafy green vegetables, such as kale, calcium-enriched juices and cereals, and tofu. A calcium supplement may be warranted if a girl gets insufficient calcium in her diet.

Mick: Are there negative psychological aspects of these disorders?

Dr. Cobb: Beyond the physical problems, disordered eating also has adverse psychological consequences. Even after resuming menses, women recovering from the female athlete triad may still struggle with issues of food and weight. If untreated, women with the female athlete triad may also go on to develop full blown eating disorders, which have a high mortality rate. Therefore, preventing disordered eating altogether is greatly preferable to treatment after the fact.

Mick: OK, Let's talk about PREVENTING the Female Athlete Triad. At what age do prevention efforts need to begin?

Dr. Cobb: Girls can be at risk for developing the female athlete triad at a young age, and prevention efforts should focus on early adolescence. The majority of bone accrual occurs between the ages of 9 and 14 years. This coincides exactly with the time when girls are most at risk for developing disordered eating patterns and eating disorders. Because caloric requirements are highest when children are between 11-14 years old, restricted food intake during this period is more likely to cause energy deficiency.

Bone loss can never be completely reversed, so early diagnosis and intervention is critical. Also, it should be noted, that an analog to the female athlete triad (disordered eating, low sex steroids, and low bone strength) may exist in males, but this has not yet been established.

PREVENTION OF THE FEMALE ATHLETE TRIAD
1. EDUCATION

Education should aim to increase awareness of the female athlete triad and its consequences among coaches, athletes, parents, teachers, and sports physicians. Many young women are unaware of the potential harm of restrictive eating and menstrual irregularities. In one survey of college athletes, seventy percent of the women who were engaging in pathologic weight control behaviors thought this behavior was harmless. Awareness of long-term consequences might prevent girls and women from initiating these behaviors. Young runners may be more motivated by the immediate desire to prevent stress fractures and loss of training time than by the threat of early osteoporosis (which may seem very distant to a young woman).

Pre-pubertal girls should be prepared for the fact that they are going to gain weight and body fat during puberty and that this may initially affect their performance. Education efforts should attempt to dispel the myth that thinner is always better for performance. The optimal weight, for high performance, lies somewhere in between too heavy and too thin.

2. NUTRITION
Many of the nutritional messages that flood our society are geared toward the sedentary, overweight adult.

These messages promote restriction of calories and fat. These messages are not appropriate for kids who are running - especially girls who should be encouraged to eat nutrient-dense foods.

Mick: I agree that an athlete doesn't want to restrict her intake of calories. What are nutrient-dense foods?

Dr. Cobb: Nutrient-dense foods usually refer to foods that have a high amount of nutrients per calorie, as opposed to a food that is all sugar, for example.

Girls should take in adequate calories for their energy output. Eating a higher percentage of calories from fat (more fat for the same number of calories) may also help women to maintain regular menstrual periods. Adequate amounts of vitamins C, D, and K, as well as zinc and protein are also important for bone growth.

Mick: Could you more clearly describe the types of fats you recommend?

Dr. Cobb: Our study did not evaluate different types of fats in terms of their efficacy in maintaining menstruation, so, in terms of promoting menstrual regularity, all fats are probably equally effective (a donut will do!). Of course, from a cardiovascular perspective, vegetable oils, nuts, avocados, and other sources of unsaturated fats are preferable to saturated fats.

Mick: Is there a formula for calculating adequate calorie intake?

Dr. Cobb: There are calculators that can be used to estimate basal metabolic rate (based on weight, body frame size and age, plus energy expended from activity (based on the type and intensity of activity). You may be able to find one of these formulas on various on-line diet sites, but a single formula may not work well for children and teens because it depends so much on their stage of growth. The USRDA recommends about 2200 kcal per day for normal 11-18 year old girls, but this does not factor in added activity such as running. A rough guideline is to add 100 kcal per mile run per day.

Mick: Can you speak a little about calcium intake?

Dr. Cobb: While eating enough calcium (1500 mg/day) is important for bone development, eating calcium-rich foods is not sufficient to ensure bone health. Estrogen is also a key factor in building strong bones, and excess calcium will not prevent bone loss in a woman who is not menstruating or is undernourished.

Mick: How could we educate parents and athletes to ensure the proper balance of estrogen? Could you explain how to manage this?

Dr. Cobb: Estrogen balance is hard to monitor other than making sure that a woman is menstruating regularly (or gets her first period on time). Estrogen should be normal if a woman is eating right, but it's hard to give advice beyond this.

3. BONE-STIMULATING EXERCISES

High -impact exercise stimulates bone growth in children, particularly if it occurs before puberty. Therefore, exercise in childhood can help maximize peak bone density. Jumping puts higher forces on bone and stimulates more bone growth than running. Young runners should be encouraged to add jumping exercises and sports that involve jumping, such as basketball, soccer, and gymnastics, to their fitness routine.

WARNING SIGNS FOR THE FEMALE ATHLETE TRIAD

Some signs of disordered eating are:

In older girls, delayed menarche (first period) and missed menstrual periods

Restrictive eating behaviors, avoidance of certain foods

Secretive eating

Sudden weight loss or failure to make normal weight goals for age

Obsession with food and/or weight

Excessive exercise

Signs of purging

Signs of low bone strength

In older girls, delayed menarche (first period) and missed menstrual periods

Stress fractures can be a sign of low bone strength.

A bone density test is the best way to determine bone strength.

Mick: As a parent or coach, what types of annual testing would you recommend? Is there a link between low iron and these problems?

Dr. Cobb: A yearly bone density test is not necessary for most young women. A bone density test would only be recommended for women who have amenorrhea, fractures, or an overt eating disorder. Low iron may reflect nutritional deficiencies, but low iron per se does not have a large effect on bone health.

Mick: Did you read the section on kidsrunning.com on "What the elites eat?" What do you think of that series?

Dr. Cobb: This looks great; it's especially good for young women to see that elite women athletes eat a full lunch that includes high-calorie and high-fat foods like nuts and peanut butter and cookies, as well as dairy foods such as yogurt.

Kristin Cobb does research on the female athlete triad at Stanford University. She used to compete in track and cross country in New England, but now just runs leisurely on the sunny trails of California.

1999 Hershey's North American Final medal winners
Chantelle Dron, Russell Brown, Michael Grant
Courtesy photo, Mick Grant

Keely Maguire, Alanna Poretta, Mick Grant,
Eric McDonald, Dan Wang
Courtesy photo, Mick Grant

F. WRAP-UP, A FEW FINAL THOUGHTS
38. COMMON MYTHS AND MISCONCEPTIONS

1) <u>Youth Athletes Should Do No Routine Training Until Age 14</u>: Youth coaches and former youth athletes and any East African champion who ran several miles to and from school each day know this is a silly misconception. However, the misconception is widely accepted in the American running community. In EVERY other sport it is well known and accepted that it is not only ok to formally start early, but that you MUST start early or you will be at a huge, if not prohibitive disadvantage. In football kids start Pop Warner at age 5 with practices up to 2 hours. Most kids in America now start youth soccer at age 5 or even younger. Nearly every champion golfer, tennis player, and gymnast started formal practice by age 5. Tiger Woods started at age 3. The Williams sisters started tennis formally at age 5. The same for swimming, where Michael Phelps started at age 6 and was a national age group record setter by age 9. Swimmer Missy Franklin started swimming at age 5. Mary Cain started competitive swimming at a young age and switched to competitive running and ran a 5:47 mile at age 11. Jenny Simpson who won a gold medal and a silver medal in the 1500 started training at age 7. The two greatest distance runners of all time are Haile Gebrselassie and Kenenisa Bekele. Like the vast majority of East African champions, they started routine training at age 5. They both said that they ran to and from school as children. Haile told Mick that he ran 10 kilometers each way (6.2 miles each way) and Kenenisa said that he "only" had to run 5 kilometers each way (3.1 miles each way). By the time they reached age 14, which is when misinformed Americans say you should start routine training, Haile already had about 20,000 lifetime accumulated miles, a total most serious Westerner distance runners don't reach until early to mid 20s. Olympic Champion and WR setting marathoner Sammy Wanjiru got a "late start" by Kenyan standards waiting until age 8 to start significant running. By age 14, before most Americans even start training, he came close to breaking 14 minutes for 5000. Sebastian Coe, the first runner to run 1:41 for the 800, started being trained by his father at age 11. In America, parents seem to respect sports like football, soccer, swimming, tennis, golf etc. and by respect, I mean they know that to be really successful, you have to start at an early age with significant practice, or you will be way behind, even hopelessly behind similarly talented kids, and therefore, they

encourage and sign their kids up for these other sports. For some reason that same respect doesn't apply to running, where it is assumed that if you start 4-6 years later it will make no difference. This widely accepted misconception has handicapped American distance running to the point where no American men won a single Olympic or World Championship medal in the 10000 for 48 years between 1964 and 2012, and for example, only one American man ranked in the top 50 times in the marathon in 2011, a list dominated by African born runners who started running at a young age.

2) <u>Mileage Burns Out Runners</u>: This misconception didn't exist until the early and mid '80s when certain mainstream running magazines began pushing "Quality over Quantity" and "Less Is More". The misconception has decreased in recent years, but there are still way too many people holding onto this misconception. What burns out runners is too many races and/or too much hard interval training carried on for too long. The lactic acid from these puts significant stress on the Central Nervous System and can result in burnout when carried on for too many weeks. Running aerobic mileage, on the other hand, has just the opposite effect, as it produces a pleasantly tired feeling due to the production of endorphins, which produce a feeling of well-being during the run, and the effect lasts for a couple of hours after the run, and is commonly referred to as "The Runner's High". Sustained aerobic running also increases serotonin production, which is necessary for humans to have a feeling of happiness, well-being, and to ward off depression. So aerobic mileage not only doesn't burn you out, it does the opposite, and makes you want even more. Also, note that working on basic speed by doing short sprints with long recoveries such that no lactic acid is accumulated, will not burn you out either. Do not confuse mileage, which will never burn you out, with too much anaerobic racing and workouts, which will burn you out. See **Chapter 10** for more information.

3) <u>Running Too Much Mileage Will Make You Slower</u>: This widely held misconception exists because people don't understand the cause and effect. They see examples over and over where athletes do a long relatively high mileage base phase, and then when the athlete gets on the track, they find out they have indeed lost some speed. They immediately conclude "all that mileage made them slower". They are missing the cause and effect. All the mileage they did had no effect positive or negative on their speed. The reason they got slower is they

went several months without doing any basic speed training. Even if they did zero mileage during that time, they would have lost the exact same amount of speed. It is the basic principle of "use it or lose it." That is what differentiates our coaching and this book from most coaching methods and other books, in that during the aerobic mileage base phase, we work on basic speed most of the year. See **Chapter 14** for more information. Also be aware that every 5 years or so entrepreneurs/personal trainers will be coming out with "new" "revolutionary" training programs, and market them with exciting sounding names, and use attractive models to advertise them. These fads will be popular for a few years, but there is nothing new about them; they are just a newly packaged version of "less is more" anaerobic interval training under a new name, and being sold for big bucks to a new group of unsuspecting people, looking for an illusorily shortcut.

4) <u>It Is Good To Be Aerobically Under-Trained By A Low Mileage Program In High School</u>: It actually IS good for sharp eyed college coaches to spot and recruit such runners for their school. It is good for the coach, because they can get you for a "cheaper price" than you deserve. Being aerobically under-trained in a low mileage program could lead to not getting into your #1 college choice and not getting the scholarship and/or financial aid grant money you could have otherwise gotten.

The truth is more like, for better or worse, being in better shape usually means running faster times, and that means you have a better chance to get into your #1 college choice and with more scholarship and/or financial aid grant money.

Another reason to **not** be aerobically under-trained in high school is that it will take less time to reach your full potential.

Another reason to **not** be aerobically under-trained is that you won't initially have sufficient base to train at the college level, and your college coach may try to rush things, resulting in injury. You should run to have fun, stay healthy, and enjoy the experience, but it is a fact that if you reach high enough level in high school, your running could make a difference in getting into and paying less at the college of your choice. The better you are in high school, the more likely you will be recruited by a college coach, which can help a student/athlete get into a better reach school, in many cases, because of the combination of academic and athletic performance. It is no coincidence that the vast majority of Mick's athletes wound up at outstanding colleges as explained in **the Foreword** to this book.

In conclusion, it is great for eagle eyed college coaches to get you for a "cheaper price", if you are under-trained aerobically in a low mileage high school program, but it is not good for you. On the other hand, it IS good for you to be under-raced and to do less heavy anaerobic training in high school.

5) <u>Running A Lot of Miles as a Youth Will Limit Your Ultimate Potential</u>: If this were true, the East Africans would not be dominating the middle distances and distances every year; the Americans would be dominating, but we know the opposite is true. Running a lot of miles won't limit your ultimate potential, but if your mileage were absurdly high as a youth, you could get to that ultimate potential sooner, but it is extraordinarily rare. Even Gerry Lindgren, who claims to have run more miles in high school than anyone in history, improved in college. High mileage high school runners such as Chris Solinsky and Dathan Ritzenhein improved dramatically in college and beyond. To reach your full potential, you have to run 15,000 to 20000 or more lifetime accumulated aerobic miles. The highest mileage high school programs don't reach these numbers, and if you follow the guidelines in this book, you won't come near those numbers in high school. See **Chapter 8** for more information.

6) <u>Lydiard Advocated Long Slow Distance LSD</u>: Lydiard did not advocate long slow distance, he advocated running at a strong aerobic pace during his base phase. He also advocated doing 1 or 2 "three quarter effort" runs per week or what we now call "tempo" runs. This misconception will apparently go on forever. See **Chapter 6** for a summary of Lydiard's Principles.

39. COMMON MISTAKES TO AVOID

1) <u>Don't run too many races</u>: If you are tired of reading this message in the book, then we have done our job. You don't get better by running a ton of races, you get better by training. Resist the temptation to over-race. Be wary of people who whenever they see a race scheduled on a calendar say "you should run this race". Races are fun and exciting and suspenseful for parents and coaches standing on the sidelines WATCHING, but excessive racing will burn you out. Running aerobic miles is putting money in the bank, and running races is taking money out of the bank. Spend your money wisely. Follow the guidelines outlined in **Chapter 21**.

2) <u>Don't do too much anaerobic interval training</u>: If you are tired of reading this message in the book, then we have done our job. Anaerobic interval training is necessary to race at your best, but the results are only temporary, and it can result in burnout if overdone. Running aerobic miles is putting money in the bank, and running races and anaerobic interval training is taking money out of the bank. Spend your money wisely. Follow the guidelines outlined in **Chapter 10**.

3) <u>Don't take the fun out of running</u>: The overriding principle of this book is **_FUN FIRST_**. Running is good for the mind, body, and spirit and it should be something you do for the rest of your life, and a major positive in your life. Don't ruin it by taking the fun out of it. The competition part of running should be just a part of your running experience. You want to enjoy the whole process. Most of the mistakes people make that take the fun out of running are related to competition. Too many races and too much anaerobic interval training are the top causes of burnout, and the leading cause of kids quitting the sport. Unrealistic goal setting can also spoil the fun. See **Chapter 19** on proper goal setting. Too much emphasis on winning can ruin the fun. If you follow the guidelines of this book, you should try to win any race you can possibly win, but never obsess over winning, nor obsess over the results of any race. You can't control what other runners do, you can't control their training, you can't control who will show up for any given race, you can't control how they feel on that day, you can only control yourself. The focus should be on your own improvement each year. It is possible to make the Olympics without ever winning a race, but it is impossible to get anywhere near a world-class level, no matter how many races you win, unless you

continuously improve year after year, after year. Another fun killer is the overzealous parent (see below).

4) <u>Don't be an overzealous parent</u>: The overzealous parent will not only kill the fun for the athlete, but they will hurt the progress of the athlete, and eventually drive both the kid and the parent away from the sport, and leave a bitter tastes in both mouths. The overzealous parent may appear on the surface to be passionate about the sport, but in reality they lack respect for the sport, which will be exhibited by their behaviors, which are listed below. If you are, or are becoming an overzealous parent by exhibiting one or more of the traits below, you need to change your behavior immediately, or you will ruin the fun for your kid, and their running career. If you are coaching an athlete with an overzealous parent, you need to try to educate the parent, or insulate the kid as best you can, but be forewarned these situations usually end badly. Here are the traits of the overzealous parent:

- You know a little about running, but you don't realize how little you know, and that a little knowledge is dangerous, much more dangerous than a parent who knows nothing, and knows they know nothing.
- You have no interest in learning anything new by reading (such as this book), and studying the methods of successful coaches, because you feel you already know everything.
- You have never coached middle and distance runners yourself, but you feel you already know everything.
- You want your kid to run as many races as possible, because it is fun and exciting for you to WATCH.
- You don't understand the connection between training and race performance, and you think running races is like spinning a roulette wheel, and the more you spin, the more likely a miraculous performance will suddenly happen.
- You notice that anaerobic interval training seems to give quick results, so you think your kid should be doing that all the time.
- You think that your kid should always "get out fast" in every race and try to run the competition into the ground, and if not, hang on as long as possible, no matter what the race distance, the competition, your kid's fitness, the relative importance of the race, the weather conditions, etc. The strategy is always the same, because you believe it is impossible or too tough to pass people.

- You are primarily focused on winning alone, and not focused too much on times or improvement. No matter how fast your kid runs, you will always be at least a little disappointed if they didn't win.
- While all parents are biased to some extent towards their own children and less objective, you think your kid is much better than they really are. You think your kid is special and will win just because they are special. You also greatly underestimate how many rungs there are on the ladder from the bottom to the top and think your child has only a few more rungs to go, when in reality, they are not even close. This results in unrealistic goals and expectations, pressure on your kid, and frequent failure and disappointment.
-You treat every race like it is a life or death matter, and put too much pressure on the kid, and make them tense before and during races, which hurts their performance.
-During races you yell out false information like "you can catch them!!" or you "can still get a great time!" even when there is no hope of that happening.
- You are always complaining about effort of athletes at races. Either saying "my kid is the only one on the team who is trying" or criticizing your own kid's lack of effort such as "Why did you just let them pass you?!!" After every race, lack of effort will always be a major complaint by the overzealous parent.

5) Failure to work on basic speed: This is a nearly universal problem in America. You should be working on basic speed most of the year, because this determines your ultimate potential in the middle distances and your ability to outkick runners at the end of races. Many coaches think anaerobic interval training improves basic speed but it does not. Others think run of the mill striders improve basic speed but they do not. See **Chapter 14** for the correct way to work on basic speed.

6) Letting small injuries to become big injuries: If you ignore a tiny pain and just hope it goes away, it could lead to a show stopping injury. Don't let it get that far. Immediately discontinue running, have an expert assess the injury, and treat the injury. See **Chapter 30** for injury prevention and **Chapter 31** for injury treatment.

7) Putting youth runners into long distance races: You don't want to put young kids immediately into 5K and 10K road races, even if they are good at them. It will retard their long term development. You need to start young kids literally in the sprints such as the 100 and 200, and gradually move them up to the 400, and later the 800, and later the

mile. They need to learn to race at the shorter distances, and improve their basic speed, and only gradually over the years, move up in race distances. This is the ideal for best long term results. See **Chapter 2** for more information on this topic.

8) <u>Not encouraging young kids to run</u>: As explained in the misconceptions section above, Americans believe young kids should start all sports at a young age EXCEPT running. If a kid likes running and is interested in running, encourage them to start running. If you or another family member runs, have them run the first part of the run with you. As long as they enjoy it and are healthy, have them keep doing it, and gradually increase their running following the guidelines in **Chapter 8**. Starting them early, gives them a huge advantage over other kids of similar talent who are not running.

9) <u>Trying to copy the training of elite professional runners or coaches who train elite professional runners</u>: In practice it makes perfect sense; why not copy what the best of the best are doing? Here is why you should not. Firstly, what they are doing right now, which is what they and their coaches will talk about in interviews, is completely irrelevant to how they developed from a beginner to an elite level. As explained earlier in the book, whether they are East Africans who started running to and from school from age 5 onward or Westerners who started at age 14, these top of the heap athletes typically took 14 to 16 years of training to get to the top of the heap. What would be much more valuable information to you is what they did in the first 8-12 years of their training, not what they are doing right now in a special anaerobic phase, or what they used for several weeks to peak for a recent championship race. They are not going to talk about the 4 miles to and from school they ran every day for 10 years that developed them to a high level, because it is not as exciting as some specific phase of complicated and high tech sounding anaerobic workouts they have used the last few weeks to peak for a race. Secondly, all of these athletes all have 15,000 to 20,000 or more lifetime accumulated miles, before they started doing the special anaerobic phase training they are doing now, and talking about in their interviews. High school runners with puny lifetime accumulated miles in the 3000 to 6000 range and their coaches, read these articles by the pros, and their pro coaches, and think they will benefit from these pros' workouts, and they don't understand that without the huge, lifetime aerobic base, these workouts are useless or worse for them. These

articles are not about how to actually develop runners, which this book is about; these articles don't bake the cake, they only address putting the frosting on the cake; they don't tell you how to bake the cake. Thirdly, to make it to the top of the heap in the world requires extraordinary innate talent, light years away from the talent of average athletes. A large portion of what they accomplished came from talent, and following their training program won't get an average runner to their level, and will likely be detrimental to the average runner. Lastly, at the elite level of any sport you enter the realm where Performance Enhancing Drugs (PEDs) may be used in some circles. In the 1970s and 1980s, a tiny country produced scores of Olympic and World Championship medalists and top 10 World Rankers every year in the middle and long distances. Everyone was trying to find out and copy their training secrets. Only decades later, was it discovered that they had a systematic PED program, and if you followed their training methods, it would have been a disaster for you, because you wouldn't have had the recovery ability they had while using their PEDs. Any time you are reading articles on the training of the very best in the world, unfortunately, you can never be sure exactly what they are doing. In summary, if you are still a developing athlete with way less than 15000 to 20000 lifetime accumulated aerobic miles, the training that a pro coach is talking about, or the best in the world athlete is doing right now in for example the 14th year of the 14 years of training they have done in their lifetime, is completely irrelevant and useless, or worse to a developing athlete.

10) <u>Don't waste time searching the internet for relative low mileage success stories</u>: It is human nature to try to find an easy solution to something that is challenging, or to find a shortcut to accomplish a goal and expend less time and energy. At any time, you can go onto a running related message board, and find the kid who is desperately searching for relative low mileage success stories, and loudly trumpeting the few they have found, and trying to debate and convince anyone who will listen to the wisdom they discovered, and of course they are actually subliminally trying to convince themselves. Their time would be much better spent out actually running aerobic miles, rather than searching for relative low mileage success stories. The truth of the matter is, consistently running aerobic miles is like putting money in the bank, and it compounds in improvement year after year just like interest. You won't find diminishing returns from running aerobic mileage until you reach at least 15,000 to 20,000 lifetime

accumulated miles, and some continue to improve even after reaching 30000 lifetime accumulated miles. Sure you can always find super talented individuals, who had great success in high school off of relatively low mileage, but if you examine all the legendary high school programs that have had top 10 in the country XC team ranking runs for 5 years or more, that is where you get useful data, because it factors out the rare exceptional individual talent data points. These programs always run higher relative mileage than the average high school program. Even pointing out famous individual runners who apparently succeeded on low relative mileage is misleading. For example, Bernard Lagat is frequently cited as a "low mileage" example success story with his training being in the 70 mpw range, which is significantly below your typical Olympic/World Championship medalist in the 5000 meters. What they don't realize is, for example, when Lagat set his lifetime best of 12:53.60 for 5000 in 2011, he had already been training consistently for more than 25 years. His lifetime accumulated miles by 2011 was likely in excess of 60,000 miles. This means it is preposterous for an 18 year old who hopes to come close to his full potential in the next few years, if he is doing about 60 MPW with 8000 lifetime accumulated miles, and thinking he can compare that to a Bernard Lagat doing 60 MPW but with 60,000+ lifetime accumulated miles. Another frequently used and misleading example is Sebastian Coe. Coe and his father and coach Peter both liked to stress that he rarely ran more than 60 MPW and was closer to 50 most of the time. Peter liked to say that they would do the minimum to produce results. However, Coe started formal training at age 11 and didn't set his personal best in the 800 of 1:41.73 until age 25, and 1500 best of 3:29.77 (worth 3:46.78 for the mile) until age 30. Therefore Coe had been training for 14 years before his 800 best, and 19 years before his 1500/mile best. Coe likely had over 30,000 lifetime accumulated miles when he ran his 800 best in 1981, and over 40,000 lifetime accumulated miles before he ran his 1500/mile personal best in 1986. So that minimum amount Peter Coe talked about turns out to be quite a large amount. So the two prime low MPW guys people like to use as examples, and then preach the virtue of low mileage, actually had massive accumulated lifetime mileage, when they ran their lifetime bests. In summary, spend your time building and accumulating aerobic mileage as outlined in **Chapter 8**, instead of searching for low mileage success stories on the internet.

11) Don't make practices too long: This is not saying don't run a lot. It is saying don't have lots of wasted dead time at practice. Focus on actual training which is most important. Limit speeches and other dead time and long drawn out stretching. If you make practices too long, you will lose some kids who think the time commitment is too much. One of the beauties of our sport is you can reach your full potential, while devoting just a fraction of the time most other sports require to reach your full potential, such as swimming, football, gymnastics, soccer, basketball, baseball, any "team sport", tennis, etc. I can't think of any other sport that requires less total time per day to reach full potential. Take advantage of this fact and don't unnecessarily waste this advantage with too many speeches and dead time at practice.

12) Choosing Inappropriate Role Models: A common mistake by runners is to choose inappropriate role models for their running. We are not talking about those who are lazy, smoke or abuse substances, etc.; those are obvious bad role models. We are talking about the highly successful runner competing in your division who is killing most of the competition off of what appears to be minimal but "smart" or "quality" training or some other efficient sounding adjective as if these runners have discovered a shortcut to success. What they are doing is considered "smart" because they are so successful. This is almost always a huge mistake for your own training.

You will constantly hear stories and see threads on running message boards talking about for example the guy who won Footlocker by only running 45 MPW or the guy who won Footlocker and barely ran during the summer and his peak mileage was 40 MPW. Both stories are mostly true. How much can you learn from their examples and successfully apply to your own running? Absolutely nothing. These people are genetic outliers and their innate talent is simply light years removed from genetically typical runners which by definition are the vast majority of us. They could have used 10 vastly different training methods and yet they still would have won or have been very close to winning or won by an even greater margin with a better training approach. At the youth and high school levels these genetic outliers can afford to make all kinds of mistakes and be significantly less fit than they could have been and still be killing the competition. The other 99.9% of us cannot afford to be making lots of mistakes and be significantly less fit than our potential to achieve any satisfying degree of success.

Even the genetic outliers have to start training properly to succeed beyond the high school level and especially at the pro level. That same 45 MPW high school champion later found that training to be woefully inadequate when he was up against equally talented professionals and he had to steadily increase his training over the years up to the 120 to 140 MPW range to allow himself to compete with his equally genetically gifted peers.

Therefore don't select randomly scattered individual success stories as role models because often their success is more due to genetics than their training programs. Some champions may be training optimally but many won't be doing optimal training and it won't work for you. You are a unique individual and as long as you are following the general guidelines of this book you and your coach or parent can successfully craft the ideal program for you. Copying the program of the best runner in your city or league or state or a Footlocker champion is likely going to be disastrous for you.

If you must to look to role models, as we previously mentioned look to the highly successful high school programs that are at or near the top over 5 or more years. You can't necessarily do that with college programs because recruiting is such a huge factor especially at the Division I level, but with high school teams the recruiting factor is eliminated. Also any high school coach can get lucky with a genetic outlier every few years, but to be successful as a team for 5 or more years in a row, they have to be doing a lot of things correctly often with kids of relatively modest talent.

40. SAMPLE TRAINING PROGRAMS

Sample 1 - Joe Molvar and Josh Molvar (Ages 6-14):
    The sample training of Coach John Molvar's sons Joe Molvar & Josh Molvar is provided below. This shows one way how the principles of this book can be applied in actual practice over several years. Joe & Josh are a good example, because they have just average talent, and it shows how the methods of this book can be used to help youth runners improve. I am fortunate to have learned so much from Mick Grant and incorporated it into my training methods which has afforded my kids an advantage over similarly average talented level kids. Throughout the sample program, we reference which chapter in the book you can refer back to for a detailed discussion on each training principle that is cited in the sample program. We caution the reader that this is just one program that follows the principles of this book. You can design your own training program for your kids that is different than this, and provided you follow the basic principles outlined in the book, you will be successful. Of course you want to design a program, but don't blindly follow it; you need to observe and adjust the program to suit your own athletes' individual needs. Pay attention and make sure they are responding positively to the stimulus of the training. Most importantly the overriding principle of the book is have fun and stay healthy!

2006
Joe is age 7 and Josh is age 6. In the spring they asked if they could run with their mother and not only did we say yes, we encouraged them to do so. (See **Chapters 36 and 37** on avoiding the mistake of not encouraging young kids to run.) They loved it right from the start and quickly became hooked on running and remain so to this day. (See **Chapter 1** on the **FUN FIRST** philosophy of this book.) Joe and Josh started running with their mom, Karen, about 4-6 times per week, between 1 and 2.5 miles each run, usually 2 miles. (See **Chapter 8** on how youth runners should start out from scratch.) A few weeks later I added working on basic speed training by doing repeat 40's (we used 40 yards) once a week. (See **Chapter 14** on starting kids on Basic Speed training.) They also did baseball, swimming, and gymnastics this year. (See **Chapter 2** on not limiting young kids to only running.) For the year, they ran 0 races, did 0 anaerobic training, but did put about 500 aerobic miles in the bank and worked on improving basic speed most of the year. (See **Chapter 10** on limiting anaerobic

training for youths and **Chapter 21** on limiting races so kids don't burn out.) Looking back, I probably should have had them run a few youth sprint races at 50 to 200 meters. (See **Chapter 2** on how you should start kids out doing sprint races.)

2007

Joe is age 8 and Josh is age 7. They ran 7 days a week. They stopped running with mom because she was too slow to keep up with them, and they just ran together always first thing in the morning. Neither myself nor their mom oversaw their runs; they ran at their own pace on their own. Most of their distance runs are done before I even wake up in the morning. (See **Chapter 37** on the pitfalls of becoming an overzealous parent.) On 5 days a week, they went 2 miles, and one day, they did a long run of 3 miles. (**See Chapter 8** on increasing mileage and adding a long run). One day they did a tempo run of 2 miles. They started out at about 15:30 and by year end, best time for Joe was 14:05 and Josh 14:17. (See **Chapter 9** on Tempo runs). They continued to do repeat 40's once a week to work on basic speed. With a flying start (See **Chapter 14**), they started the year at about 6.7 and improved to about 6.0 for Josh, and 6.1 for Joe for 40 yards. When the track was covered in snow, we used a flat stretch of road with low traffic and good sun exposure. (See **Chapter 17** on improvising and overcoming obstacles). They lost interest in baseball and gymnastics, but continued to do swimming and added backyard football to their playtime. They also joined Cub Scouts. For the year they ran 0 races, did 0 anaerobic training, but did put about 750 aerobic miles in the bank and worked on improving basic speed the entire year. Looking back I probably should have had them run a few youth sprint races at 50 to 200 meters.

2008

Joe is age 9 and Josh is age 8. They continued to run 2 miles a day, with one tempo or faster 2 mile on Friday, and Saturday they did a 3 mile long run. They continued to work on basic speed most of the year, improving their 40Y time from the 6.0/6.1 to the 5.7/5.8 range. This routine was continued the whole year. They did however run one mile race, the High Street Mile. We did no anaerobic interval training, since they were prepubescent kids (See **Chapter 10**); instead they did a 400 time trial 10 days before the race in 80-82, an 800 time trial 7 days before the race in 2:58-2:59 and a 1200 time trial 4 days before the race in 4:34-4:38. We set a goal of 6:04 for Joe and 6:12 for Josh.

(See **Chapter 19** for goal setting). I gave them their splits every 200 to keep them on pace (see **Chapter 20** for proper pacing in races). Joe ran 6:00 and won the age 9 and under category, and Josh ran 6:07 and was 2nd in the 9 and under category. They continued to do swimming, Cub Scouts and backyard football, and added backyard basketball to their play routines. They also added formal tennis lessons. For the year, they ran 1 race, did 0 anaerobic training, but did put another 750 aerobic miles in the bank and worked on improving basic speed the entire year. Looking back, I probably should have had them run a few youth sprint races at 50 to 200 meters.

2009

Joe is age 10 and Josh is age 9. They continued to run 2 miles a day, with one tempo or faster 2 mile on Friday and a long run on Saturday. The one change is they increased the long run from 3 to 4 miles. They continued to work on basic speed most of the year improving their 40 time from the 5.7/5.8 to 5.5/5.6 range. They improved their 2 mile tempo run times to about 12:20 for Joe and about 12:40 for Josh. This routine was continued the whole year. Again they ran one mile race, the High Street Mile. We did no anaerobic interval training, since they were prepubescent kids; instead they did a 400 time trial 10 days before the race in 77, an 800 time trial 7 days before the race in 2:48, and a 1200 time trial 4 days before the race in 4:18. We set a goal of 5:48 for both of them. I gave them their splits every 200 to keep them on pace (see **Chapter 20** for proper pacing in races). Joe ran 5:45 and won the 10-12 age category, missing the record by 8 seconds, and Josh ran 5:46 and won the 9 and under category, breaking the record that had stood for 13 years, by 5 seconds. Although they tried to win and won their age categories, the primary focus is improving, setting realistic goals, and proper pacing by hitting splits; winning is only a secondary focus. (See **Chapter 37** on avoiding common mistakes by overzealous parents such as excessive focus on winning.) They continued to do swimming, tennis, Cub Scouts, backyard football, and backyard basketball in their play routines. For the year, they ran 1 race, did 0 anaerobic training, but did put another 825 aerobic miles in the bank, and worked on improving basic speed the entire year. Looking back, I probably should have had them run a few youth sprint races at 50 to 200 meters.

2010

Joe is age 11 and Josh is age 10. They continued the same routine as the previous year. However, this was a mistake, because I was very busy this year, and had very little oversite over their running, and we didn't get the tempo runs done. I failed to pay close enough attention to see if they were responding positively to the training, as we talked about in the book. The result was they made only a little progress as far as building endurance and basic speed that year. At the High Street Mile that year, they improved to 5:39, taking 1-2 in the 10-12 age group and missing the record by 2 seconds. After the race, they told me they wanted to increase their running a lot and get much better. (See **Chapter 18** on moving up to the next level.) For the year, they ran 1 race, did 0 anaerobic training, but did put another 825 aerobic miles in the bank.

2011

Joe is age 12 and Josh is age 11. They increased their running to 19 MPW by doing alternating 2 and 3 miles runs and doing a 4 mile long run (See **Chapter 8** on increasing mileage). They continued to do repeat 40's once a week, but added a second basic speed work a second day a week, adding repeat 200's. (See **Chapter 14** on using 200's for basic speed endurance). They continued with a 2 mile tempo run once a week. The result was dramatic improvement, the biggest one year improvement since they started running. This is what their routine looked like:

M 2 easy
Tu 3 easy
W 2 easy plus 5 x 40 (walk back recovery)
Th 3 easy
F 2 mile tempo run
Sa 2 easy
Su 4 easy plus 5 x 200 (100 walk/100 jog)
Total 19 mpw

For the 200's, they started at 45 and improved to the 33-34 range by the end of the year. For repeat 40's, Josh improved to the 5.3 range and Joe to about 5.6 range for 40 yards. It became clear that Josh has better natural speed than Joe. Their 2 mile tempos improved to the 11:50's range. Again, they did no anaerobic training the whole year and ran one race the High Street Mile, with only the 3 time trials in the last 10 days, where they ran 400 (68-69), 800 (2:30-2:31), and 1200

(3:59). We set a goal of 5:20 for both. In the race, Joe ran 5:20, winning the 10-12 age group and breaking the record which had stood for 11 years, by 16 seconds, and Josh ran 5:21, taking 2nd in the age group, and also 15 seconds under the old record. After the race, the boys were ecstatic and loving running more than ever. Following the principles of this book, they are having fun and staying healthy (See **Section E** for Injury Prevention) and training consistently, which is a recipe for great progress despite their limited innate talent. They were so enthusiastic, they wanted to significantly increase their training. (See **Chapter 18** on moving up to the next level.) So over the next 12 months, I gradually increased their mileage step by step. They continued to do swimming and tennis and had now crossed over to Boy Scouts and did backyard football and backyard basketball in their play routines. For the year, they ran 1 race, did 0 anaerobic training, but did put another 950 aerobic miles in the bank and worked on improving basic speed the entire year. Again, I probably should have had them run a few youth races at 200-800 meters.

Photo below: Josh (left) & Joe Molvar at 2011 High Street Mile.

Courtesy photo, Karen Molvar

2012
Joe is 13 and Josh is age 12. With their ever growing enthusiasm and enjoyment of the sport, and the fact they seemed to be bouncing off the walls with energy, and the fact they wanted to do more, I gradually increased their training, which by half way through the year, consisted of this routine:

M 5 easy
Tu 3 x 1 mile (4 min jog) at high aerobic effort, not anaerobic effort
W AM: 5 easy PM: 5 x 40 (walk back for full recovery)

Th 5 easy
F   3 mile tempo
Sa 5 easy
Su AM: 5 easy   PM: 5 x 200 (100 walk/100 jog resulting in full recovery)
Total 35 mpw

As you can see, I increased their tempo run from 2M to 3M and added a second tempo run of 3 x 1 mile. To shake things up, I would occasionally substitute 1.5M tempos, and once in a while, 3 x 800 tempos, but carefully monitoring their effort and their HR (See **Chapters 9 and 16** for proper utilization of HR data), and verifying they were responding positively to the training (See **Chapter 9**). I also introduced a short 10 minute weight training program to their routine, to also help improve basic speed (See **Chapter 33**). Indeed they responded very well to the overall program, with their biggest one year improvement ever. In the repeat 40's, Josh improved to the 4.9 range and Joe to the 5.3 range for 40 yards. In the 200's, they improved to 31-32. In the 3M tempos, they started out at the 19:50's range and improved to the 17:40's range. In June, Joe (age 13), and Josh (age 12), finished 1-2 in a tactical race at the Hershey Massachusetts State Championship 800 boys "13-14" age group. In August at the High Street Mile, I set a goal of 5:00 for both of them, and as always gave them splits at every 200 to keep them on pace, and Joe ran 4:57, breaking none other than Mick Grant's son Michael Grant's age 13 record for that race by 3 seconds, which was a record that had stood for more than 10 years. Josh ran 5:02, breaking Joe's record for the 10-12 age group from the previous year, by 19 seconds. Needless to say, following the principles of this book, Joe and Josh are having a lot of fun, and are staying healthy, and are consequently improving. They have now been running for 7 years and neither has had a single injury. Their enthusiasm seems to grow every year. They are still heavily involved in Boy Scouts with a goal of attaining Eagle Scout, and play lots of backyard football and basketball. They stopped formal swim and tennis lessons, but still enjoy swimming at the beach and playing tennis regularly. The plan going forward is of course more of the same, continue to put money in the bank, i.e. build endurance, which is the key to long term improvement (see **Chapter 4**), by gradually increasing mileage, and doing long runs, and doing 2 tempos runs per week, and to continue to improve basic speed, by doing repeat 40's and 200's. Josh plans to do the Junior Olympics XC series this fall and Hershey T&F meets next year. Joe will be running for his local high school team as a freshman and will be incorporating the guidelines for dealing with the excessive high school race schedule. (See the end of **Chapter 21** for guidelines in dealing with the excessive high school race schedule, so that you can still follow the principles of this book, while running for your local high school).

Photo Below: Joe (age 13) & Josh (age 12) taking 1st and 2nd in a tactical 800 "Age 13-14" at the Hershey Massachusetts State Track Championship.

Courtesy photo, Karen Molvar

Photo Below: Joe (age 13, 4:57) & Josh (age 12, 5:02), after the 2012 High Street Mile.

Courtesy photo, Karen Molvar

Mid Nov 2012 XC Update: The plan for Joe was quite successful. He was faced with a daunting 15 meet XC schedule so he followed the plan outlined in **Chapter 21** of the book. So we picked the 4 most important meets (final home dual meet, league meet, State Division meet and All State Meet) to run all out and the other 11 meets were run at 3/4 effort tempo pace as part of his training including the NXN Regional meet (photo below). All team interval workouts before Oct 10th were run at high aerobic tempo effort and the ones after Oct 10th leading up to the championships were run anaerobically which allowed him to stay healthy and peak perfectly for the big meets and have lots of fun all season. In the final dual meet on his home course he ran the fastest time ever by a freshman in the 26 year history of the course. He placed 8th in his league meet and tied for the fastest time ever run by a freshman in that meet. He placed 13th in his state divisional meet in 16:48 on a legit 5K XC course. He placed 56th in his All State meet. He was 3rd man on a Newburyport High School team that went undefeated in dual meets, won the league meet, won the state divisional meet and finished 3rd in the All State meet.

Photo of Joe Molvar. **Courtesy photo, Karen Conway**

Josh had an equally successful XC season. Because he wasn't running for a team and running unattached we could pick his races and limit his races so he would only run 5 of them and run all of them all out. He was able to delay starting his anaerobic phase until right before his first race so he could peak for the big races and it allowed for a nice long base phase in the fall to maximize his long term improvement. He was Massachusetts 8th grade state XC champion in meet record time as a 12 year old. Then on his birthday he placed 3rd in the New England Junior Olympics Championship (Age 13-14) and was 1st among 13 year olds and then placed 11th in the Northeast Region I Junior Olympics Championship and was 2nd among 13 year olds and qualified for the Nationals.

Josh Molvar taking 3rd at New Englands. **Courtesy photo, Karen Molvar**

The plan going forward is of course more of the same, continue to put money in the bank, i.e. build endurance, which is the key to long term improvement (see **Chapter 4**), by gradually increasing mileage, and doing long runs, and doing 2 tempos runs per week, and to continue to improve basic speed, by doing repeat 40's and 200's. Joe and Josh will only run 1-2 indoor races unattached just for fun (see **Chapter 7**) and in the spring Joe will rejoin his high school team for outdoor track and will be incorporating the guidelines for dealing with the excessive high school race schedule. (See the end of **Chapter 21** for guidelines in dealing with the excessive high school race schedule, so that you can still follow the principles of this book, while running for your local high school). Josh plans to do the Hershey T&F meets during the outdoor season. For the year 2012 they both ran a total of 8 all out races, did a total of about 6 weeks of anaerobic work and about 46 weeks of aerobic base training. They ran a total of about 2100 aerobic miles for the full year bringing their lifetime accumulated total to about 6700 miles.   As stated previously in the book, it takes a minimum of about 15,000-20,000 lifetime accumulated miles to reach your full potential and some people continue to improve up to 30,000.

2013

Joe is 14 and Josh is 13. Using the principles in the book, Joe & Josh have been able to make solid progress since XC ended. Their training was uninterrupted by illness, not even a single cold the entire winter. For December through March, I used the following training pattern which they responded to very well. It is a simple 3 day cycle incorporating everything from this book:

Day 1: AM: 5M Easy

PM: Work on basic speed (*see below)

Day 2: Tempo Run **(see below)

Day 3: 10M easy long run

Then repeat the cycle over and over again.

It totaled 45-50 MPW, with 2 or 3 tempos per week and 2 or 3 times working on basic speed per week. There were always 2 easy distance days between each tempo and always 2 days between each basic speed session. There was zero anaerobic interval training and only 1 low key race. Nothing was done on a track which was buried in snow and ice all winter anyway. We used wheeled off sections of flat roads for the tempos and basic speed stuff.

*The basic speed work on day 1 alternated between these 2 workouts. Note that for both, this is not anaerobic interval training, it is alactic basic speed workout with long recoveries and short stuff so no lactic acid accumulates.

basic speed one: 5 x 40 (3 min recovery) for raw speed development

basic speed two: 5 x 200 (full recovery which for them is 100 walk/100 jog) for speed endurance development.

** The tempos rotated between 3 different tempos:

Tempo 1: 3M continuous tempo

Tempo 2: segmented tempo of 3 x 1 mile (800 jog recovery) Note this is not a traditional 3 x 1 mile anaerobic workout, it is done at a much lower effort so it stays in high aerobic range.

Tempo 3: segmented tempo of 4 x 800 (400 jog recovery) Note this is not a traditional 4 x 800 anaerobic workout, which is done at a much lower effort so it stays in high aerobic range.

As you can see above in this simple program they are constantly hitting every pace you can imagine from all out 40 sprint up through easy long run and yet the program is designed such they do not go anaerobic. By late March they improved the 3M tempos by 2:00 faster than they were running the year before at this time and 1:00 faster than they were on Labor Day just before XC started. This base work resulted in an outstanding freshman track season for Joe when he rejoined his local high school team in April. He improved his 800 PR from 2:23 to 2:14 (after running a mile an hour earlier), his mile PR from 4:57 to 4:45 and he broke the 42 year old freshman school and league record in the 2 mile running 10:00 and peaked perfectly for the championship races placing 3rd in his league meet and 6th in his state divisional meet in the 2 mile. We managed his difficult 15 meet schedule by only running 5-6 races all out and used the other 9-10 races as tempo efforts so he wouldn't burn out or peak too early.

Joe Molvar, freshman outdoor track. **Courtesy photo, Mary Beth Orlando**

Josh also had a solid season winning the Hershey Massachusetts State 1600 with the 2nd fastest time in the Northeast Region missing nationals by only 1 second. He also ran a personal best in the mile of 4:54 at the High Street Mile breaking his brother Joe's age 13 and under record from the year before. He also ran a personal best of 2:17 in the 800.

Josh Molvar, age 13, running 4:54 at the High Street Mile. **Courtesy photo, Karen Molvar**

Sample 2 - Chantelle Dron (Age 15-16):
The sample training of Coach Mick Grant for Chantelle Dron is provided in this secton. She is an excellent example how the principles of this book are applied to an older youth athlete. Mick started coaching the home schooled Dron when she was 10. Dron

made tremendous progress under Mick's coaching and heading into the training program below she had run a 4:53 mile winning the New Englands as a freshman. Here is her training for a full year leading up to her sensational performances including a 4:22 1500 (worth 4:43 mile):

CARL ITELLE...
CROSS COUNTRY 2002

December 12, 2002
VO2-3.709 l/min 61.3ml/kg*min

	SUN	MON	TUE	WED	THU	FRI	SAT	TOTAL	
AUG 25-31	9	4E	7	5E	1	4E	HILLS	40	13
					5:36, 5:36, 5:22				
SEPT 1-7	9	4E	LT	5E	6-7E	4E	HILLS	42	12
				WED-THU-FRI RECOVERY RUNS					
8-14	4	4E	8	5E	7	4E	0	30	11
			35:15		NO WORKOUTS				
15-21	9	E	ST	E	7	4E	HILLS	43	10
			(6:00-6:10 PACE) 5:59, 5:49, 5:41, 5:39						
22-28	9	E	E6	E	E	4E	I(5:35)	43	9
		SORE CALVES			11/2 MILE PACED RUN-WINNEKENNI (90%)				
29-OCT 5	9	E	ST	E	7	4E	G-BAY	45	8
			18:41(90%)				17:39		
6-12	9	E	E	E	E	4E	I(5:30)	45	7
							5:19, 5:18, 5:25(95%)		
13-19	9	E	LT	E	1	4E	5E	45	6
			31:15(75%)		2:31, 2:32, 2:31, 2:29(90%)				
20-26		USA TF	4	5.5	4	I(2XMILE)4E	E	35	5
HR 47		18:15			5:26, 5:20(90%)				
27-NOV2		MAYOR'S E	E	E	I(2x2K, 1X8)4E E			40	4
		18:17			1:18.01, 2:39.40, 4:02.62, 5:26.12 = 6:50.21				
					1:17.57, 2:39.22, 4:02.03, 5:23.94 = 6:43.69				
					1:15.23 = 2:30.65 (90-95%)				
3-9	9	E	ST	E	F	4E	VLASICH	40	3
			18:01(80%)				17:31		
10-16	E	E	E	E	E	1K'S 4E	E	38	2
					3:12.86, 3:12.68, 3:12.57, 3:11.82				
17-23	7	E	W/O	E	800'S	4E	E	34	1
		79/82.83/83/79 = 8:09, 85-90% EFFORT (5:27)							
		2:26.87, 2:27.17, 2:29.43, 2:29.74, 2:26.32, 90-95% HR 190-195 FOR ALL							
24-30	6	4	4	400'S	E	3E	FLNE	30	
	FELT SLUGGISH ON SUNDAY, OK ON M & T						4TH 5.23, 11.53, 18.09		
DEC1-7	E	8	E	E	W/O	4E	E	34	
HR 49					1200 3.49 (laps were between 1.15 and 1.16)				
					400's at 1.09, 1.12, 1.10, 1.08				
8-14	7	E	E	I	E	3E	FL	30	
				4 x 30 SEC 1 X 50 SEC @ MILE PACE					

ALL STEADY RUNS WILL BE OVER 6:00 PACE, ONCE A WEEK DO SOME 200'S @ 5:00 PACE
THIS IS SUBJECT TO CHANGE BASED ON HEALTH, HEARTRATE, WEATHER, ETC.
IT IS NORMAL IF WE HAVE TO ADJUST THE WORKOUTS AND/OR TIMES

WORKOUTS		
	LONG TEMPO	30-40 MINUTES @ 6:40 PACE
	SHORT TEMPO	15-20 MINUTES @ 6:00-6:10 PACE
	HILL REPEATS	GOOD FORM, STEADY PACE, SURGE OVER THE TOP
	FARTLEK	AT WILL, 4-6 MINUTE INTERVALS @ RACE PACE
	INTERVALS	VARIES BY DATE, 1 - 11/2 MILE REPEATS @ ? PACE

**CHANTELLE BROWN
INDOOR TRACK 2003**

March 12, 2003
VO2-3.709 l/min 61.3ml/kg*min

	SUN	MON	TUE	WED	THU	FRI	SAT	TOTAL	
DEC 22-28	EASY RUNNING		E	E	E	7	25-30	11
DEC 29-JAN 4	BUILD-UP PERIOD		E	E	E	2:11.1	30-35	10
	5 MILE TEMPO @ 6:30-6:40					800		
JAN 5-11	7	E	T	E	T	E	8	35-40	9
	5 MILE TEMPO @ 6:30-6:40 OR 3 MILE TEMPO @ 6:10							
JAN 12-18	3:29.6	80Bike	45Bike	4	T	E	5	40-45	8
	1200	SLIGHT SORENESS IN RIGHT FOOT, ON TOP						
JAN 19-25	4:51.62	E	6	30Bike	8	E	2:10.66	40-45	7
	SLIGHT SORENESS IN FOOT AGAIN							
JAN 26-FEB 1	7	E	9	E	I	E	7	40-45	6
					3:07, 3:08, 3:10, 3:11	BLISTERS		
					KUKINI SHOES			
FEB 2-8	90m	7	H	E	F	E	7	45	5
	BIKE						HR47		
FEB 9-15	9	E	4T@6	E	7	E	2:09.22	40	4
			HR44	4 MILE TEMPO @ 6:00 ON TREADMILL				
FEB 16-22	9	2+60B	E	10	4	4	2	30	3
		60M ON BIKE	5M @ 6:00, 2.5M @ 6:00 (47HR)					
FEB 23-MAR 1	4:53.76	E	E	I	E	49HR	E	35	2
	3x320 50.75, 51.21, 50.73	6x160 25.21, 25.35, 25.22, 25.08, 23.72						
	(The 160's felt very comfortable, so I decided to add a few more).							
MAR 2-8	3:33.03	3	E	E	I	E	I	25	1
		30.50, 30.68, 1:07.82, 1:47.79, 1:04.68, 31.11, 30.18						
MAR 9-15	6	3	I	E	I	E	E	25	
			8 X 100'S (44HR)		200'S			
MAR 16-22	NSIC (1st place 4:51.3)							

http://www.nsictf.org/nsiclead.htm

ALL STEADY RUNS WILL BE OVER 6:00 PACE, ONCE A WEEK DO SOME 200'S @ 5:00 PACE
THIS IS SUBJECT TO CHANGE BASED ON HEALTH, HEARTRATE, WEATHER, ETC.
IT IS NORMAL IF WE HAVE TO ADJUST THE WORKOUTS AND/OR TIMES

WORKOUTS	LONG TEMPO	30-40 MINUTES @ 6:40 PACE
	SHORT TEMPO	15-20 MINUTES @ 6:00-6:10 PACE
	HILL REPEATS	GOOD FORM, STEADY PACE, SURGE OVER THE TOP
	FARTLEK	AT WILL, 4-6 MINUTE INTERVALS @ RACE PACE
	INTERVALS	VARIES BY DATE, 1 - 11/2 MILE REPEATS @ ? PACE

July 3, 2003

	SUN	MON	TUE	WED	THU	FRI	SAT	TOTAL	
GENERAL FORMAT	LONG	200'S	TRAIL	EASY	TRACK	EASY	SPEED		
M16-22	NSC	E	E	E	E	E	E	20	16
M23-29	6	E	7	E	E	E	HILLS	30	15
	7-7:30/PACE (TO BE DETERMINED BY RECOVERY RATE)								
	31.56, 32.41, 32.11, 31.98, 31.98, 31.66, 31.4, 30.03								
M30-APRIL 5	9.9	E	200'S	E	TEMPO E		TEMPO 38		14
	(1:05)	HR51	HR51		5 @ 6:40		2@5:40		
	31.58, 31.38, 29.83, 30.13, 30.88, 30.58, 30.63, 29.51								
A6-12	9	E	8	E	TEMPO E		E	40	13
					3 @ 5:35 = 17:21				
A13-19	9	200's	8	E	TEMPO E		50'S	40	12
	29.61, 30.24, 30.50, 30.59, 29.84, 30.54, 30.64, 29.20								
					30:35				
A20-26	9	E	8	E	MILES E		E	40	11
					5:26, 5:21, 5:11 (4-5 MINUTES REST)				
A27-MAY3	10	E	8	E	1200'S E		50'S	30	10
	KOSMIN TEST(7520M) 4X 1200 400M REST								
	3:58.14, 3:58.59, 3:56.19, 3:53.87,								
	(1:15, 1:21, 1:22), (1:16, 1:21, 1:21), (1:18, 1:20, 1:18), (1:17, 1:18, 1:17)								
M4-10	10	200's	8	E	1000'S E		50'S	35	9
	29.63, 29.89, 30.5, 30.44, 30.89, 30.2								
	3:11.86, 3:12.11, 3:10.67, 3:10.16, 3:04.65								
	(117, 235, 311), (116, 235, 312), (116, 234, 310), (115, 234, 310), (114, 229, 304)								
M11-17	10	200'S	8	9-400's E		E	2:11	40	8
	HR57	2x200's 30.59, 30.60		69.29, 69.11, 69.27, 68.58, 69.16,					
	2x150's 22.40, 22.50			69.04, 68.54, 67.88, 65.81					
	1x300 47.69								
	2x100's 14.81, 14.60								
M18-24	9	4	200'S	E	800'S	E	RACE	38	7
	(SUB- 7) (7:00)	30.88, 30.63, 30.81, 29.68, 46.75, 14.81, 30.93, 14.92, 14.28							
	2:27.68, 2:29.54, 2:29.48, 2:23.92, 1:10.67, 1:09.46, 1:08.90, 1:07.22								
M25-31	8	200'S	7	E	I	E	2:08	36	6
							31-64-1:36		
	1:07.29, 1:52.28, 1:07.47, 1:47.08, 1:04.05, 1:42.97, 30.15								
JUNE1-7	7	150'S	7	W/O	E	E	50'S	35	5
	3X200 32.79, 30.95, 29.15								
	6X100 14.19, 14.39, 14.34, 14.36, 14.37, 14.30								
	1X400 1:04.68			800 2:25.06 35, 37, 37, 36					
				600 1:49.31 35, 38, 35					
				600 1:46.94 35, 36, 35					
				600 1:45.25 35, 35, 35					
				600 1:41.50 33, 35, 33					
				400 1:05.06 16, 16, 18, 15					
J8-14	7	150'S	7	400'S	E	E	E	35	4
	300 45.35, 200 29.44, 100 14.19, 100 14.00, 100 14.12, 400 1:04.13								
	5 X400 1:04.18, 1:04.75, 1:04.63, 1:05.69, 1:06.93								

July 3, 2003

	SUN	MON	TUE	WED	THU	FRI	SAT	TOTAL
GENERAL FORMAT	LONG	200'S	TRAIL	EASY	TRACK	EASY	SPEED	
	Golden West						USATF Junior Nationals	
J15-21	4:49.58	E	5	W	E		4:29.10	4:26.08	30	3
					600(1:38)-400(65)-200(31)-200(30)-200(34)				
J22-28	E	B	6	B	E	E	W/O	30	2
							2:18.9, 1:42.2, 65.5, 30.5		
J29-JULY 5	6	E	W/O	B	E	800T	800F	30	1
	3@6:00 PACE		46.19, 46.38, 46.82, 31.38, 30.81, 31.31						
J6-12	E	B	E	B	E	1500T	E	1500F	30
						4:22.08 Youth World Championship			

FOCUS ON RECOVERY, INCLUDE SOME STRIDES OR 150'S BASED ON HOW YOU FEEL
HAVE FUN!

J13-19	E	B	6	E	B	E	B	20

WE CAN DO SOMETHING DURING THIS WEEK, BASED ON RECOVERY

J20-26	1500F	B	E	0	0	0	0	10
	4:26 Pan Am Juniors							
J27-AUGUST2	E	E	E	B	E	E	E	15
A3-9	6	E	6	E	E	E	E	20
A10-16	7	E	7	E	E	E	E	25
A17-23	8	E	8	E	E	E	E	30
A24-30	9	E	9	T	E	E	E	35

WORKOUTS	LONG TEMPO	30-40 MINUTES @ 6:30 PACE
	SHORT TEMPO	15-20 MINUTES @ 6:00 PACE
	2 MILE TEMPO	5:50
	HILL REPEATS	GOOD FORM, STEADY PACE, SURGE OVER THE TOP
	FARTLEK	AT WILL, 4-6 MINUTE INTERVALS @ RACE PACE
	INTERVALS	VARIES BY DATE, 1 - 1 1/2 MILE REPEATS @ 5:30 PACE

41. SUMMARY OF BOOK

- "HAVE FUN!"
- Stay healthy. Be healthy enough to run every day.
- **BLACK DAYS,** Endurance training is the key to long term success.
- Focus on building endurance most of the year.
- Work on basic speed most of the year.
- **RED DAYS,** Limit heavy acid producing anaerobic training to a brief period before target race.
- Choose races wisely. Do not over race.
- Consistent training will always trump sporadic "hard training". You want to stay healthy so your training is consistent over time.
- Know what you can handle and do that in training.
- DO NOT DO WHAT YOU ARE NOT READY FOR.
- Set challenging, yet realistic short, intermediate, and long term goals.
- Consistent endurance training is money in the bank, and that is the key to long term improvement.

It is important to understand that the key to improving long term is to start (start by starting!), even if it is only one or two minutes at a time, and gradually increase the distance, in order to develop endurance. The exact same principle applies to basic speed. Whatever speed or pace our young athletes begin with is fine. The goal over time is to gradually get faster. If we have fun, stay healthy, are consistent and gradually build both endurance and basic speed, we will enjoy a rewarding running experience and improve greatly year after year.

FUN FIRST

Photo below: Russell Brown winning the 2011 Boston Indoor Games Mile over 2 Olympic medalists and the American Mile Record Holder

42. ABOUT YOUTH RUNNER MAGAZINE AND YOUTHRUNNER.COM

Youth Runner Magazine and Youthrunner.com are great resources for kids of all ages and ability levels. We have an opportunity to help the next generation of runners, along with their parents and coaches learn the fundamental skills and training methods of distance running. What we at Youth Runner do is inspire kids to be better athletes and students. Those kids usually inspire others. We give young athletes recognition that they wouldn't get anywhere else. Youth Runner offers resources for the competitive athlete and kids who just like to run. Hopefully, we are making a positive difference to kids all around the world.

43. MAJOR INFLUENCES/CREDITS

Major Influences
Arthur Lydiard
Frank Gagliano
Joe Vigil
Joe Newton
Mark Wetmore
Tony Benson
Marty Liquori
Haile Gebrselassie
Buddy Bostick
Gary Gardner
George Davis
John Parker
Lou Ristaino
Credits
Youth Runner Magazine/Youthrunner.Com
Dan Kesterson
All of Mick's Athletes
Deana Grant
Michael Grant
Sarah Grant
Jeanne Grant
Joe Molvar
Josh Molvar
Karen Molvar
Dr. Kristin Cobb
Mark Behan
Giles Norton

44. REFERENCES

RUNNING WITH LYDIARD, FIRST EDITION BY ARTHUR LYDIARD, GARTH GILMOUR, HODDER AND STOUGHTON, 1983

COACHING CROSS COUNTRY SUCCESSFULLY BY JOE NEWTON, HUMAN KINETICS, 1998

NATIONAL SLEEP FOUNDATION "THE BIOLOGY OF ADOLESCENT SLEEP" 2009-10-02

POSITION OF THE AMERICAN DIETETIC ASSOCIATION: NUTRITION AND ATHLETIC PERFORMANCE, MARCH 2009

45. MICK GRANT'S ATHLETE WILL SEIDEL DESCRIBES HIS 4 X 800 WINNING AND RECORD SETTING 2001 JUNIOR OLYMPIC EXPERIENCE

Sacramento, CA, July 2001, by Will Seidel

Above photo: Will Seidel, Mike Grant, Russell Brown, Harry Norton.
Courtesy photo, brightroom.com

This summer, during the end of July, many of the nation's Track & Field athletes gathered for the USATF Junior Olympic National Championships. Taking place in Sacramento California, this event provided many with a chance to showcase their talent during the summer months. For the past two years I have been among those competitors.

For two years I have competed as a member of Mick Grant's Whirlaway Track Club's Intermediate (15-16) Boys 4X800m relay squads. [Note Mick's Club Team was called Merrimac Valley Striders Junior Team from 1995-1997, Greater Lowell Junior Team from 1997 to 2000, Whirlaway Junior Team from 2000-2001 and Lynx Elite from 2001 to 2009.]

Courtesy photo,
brightroom.com

Other members of the two teams include Harry Norton, Mike Grant, and Russell Brown.

This year we left for California with especially high hopes. After months of training, our 4X800m team was ranked 1st in the country, having recorded a time of 8:09.12 at the regional JO qualifier. We knew that there would be tough competition, but we felt we were ready.

Not a single person on our team had suffered injury that summer, which shows the care with which we had prepared. We had trained hard, but not to the point of injury. This balance is an important one, especially for relatively young runners such as us. Since nobody had been forced to take time off because of injury, we were all in great shape.

When we finally stepped on the track, everything went right. We all ran hard, and finally broke away from the competition. As our anchor raised his arms in triumph, we all (although fatigued) found the strength to cheer. Russell had crossed the finish line in 7:56.11, more than 3 seconds faster than the previous national record of 7:59.69!

Photo above: Whirlaway Team, Finish and Relay Exchanges.
Courtesy photo, Lynx System Developers/Giles Norton

As I prepare for a season of cross-country, I doubt the memory of that victory will ever leave me. It will further motivate me to train smart, race hard, and have fun. And if you ever see me whipping through the early New Hampshire evening, on a training run, that's probably what I'm thinking about.

Thanks to Will for sharing his experience of being part of a record breaking team. And one more note. Whirlaway's anchor, Russell Brown, also won the Intermediate Boys 800m run (1:54.51).

Courtesy photo, brightroom.com

46. MICK GRANT'S SUMMARY OF HIS COACHING EXPERIENCE AT THE 2002 JUNIOR OLYMPICS

Photo of Phil Shaw, Mike Grant, Harry Norton, Tim Galebach, Russell Brown, and Will Seidel **Courtesy photo, Lynx Elite Athletics/Giles Norton**

The Lynx Elite Athletics Club coached by Mick Grant had a wonderful showing at the United States Junior Olympics National Championships in Omaha, Nebraska this week end. The Haverhill-based Lynx team qualified seven athletes to the National Championships.

The Young Men's 4 x 800 meter relay quartet are National Champions for the second consecutive year with a winning time of 7:49.82. The team is comprised of Harry Norton from North Reading, MA, Will Seidel from Newbury, NH, Mike Grant of Haverhill, MA, and Russell Brown of Hanover, NH.

Also medaling was Phil Shaw of Andover who took sixth place in the Young Men's 5k run with a great time of 16:11.69 - a race that was led, by a margin of over 30 seconds to within 40 yards of the finish line, by Tim Galebach until he collapsed from heat exhaustion and was unable to finish. (Note: the temperatures rose so high that the track surface melted in places!!!)

Katie Dlesk of Andover, who entered the National Championships seeded 34th, ran a fine 57.69 to finish 14th in the 400 meters.

The philosophy at Lynx Elite Athletics is team work and gradual improvement. In our program, we work on developing speed and mechanics while staying true to endurance development over time. It is a long term development plan and requires patience and commitment from athletes. We would rather stick with the long term plan than over train for a short term gain.

I am very proud of my athletes and am fortunate to have had them for such a long time. Our highest profile members are Chantelle Dron (4:30/1500m, 6th at USATF Junior Nationals) and the 4 x 800m relay team of Harry Norton, Will Seidel, Mike Grant, Russell Brown (1st at USATF Junior Olympics two years in a row). The 4 x 800m team has won three major championship races since 1999. I am very proud of every member of the team and am honored to have had the opportunity to work with each of them.

Photo Below: The 2002 4 x 800 National Champions.
Harry Norton, Will Seidel, Mike Grant, Russell Brown
Courtesy photo, Lynx Elite Athletics/Giles Norton

JUNIOR OLYMPICS 2003

Russell Brown, Phil Shaw, Mike Grant, and Harry Norton received Gold Medals at Junior Olympic Nationals. The quartet ended their Junior Olympic National Championship careers in grand style, winning the 4 x 800 meter relay for the third consecutive year in a time of 7:41.10. This year's race was very exciting, with many lead changes. The race was decided in a tremendous anchor leg battle between Russell Brown, of Lynx Elite, and Davon Johnson, of Florida City Parks and Recreation.

Back Cover of Book/Book Description

The Youth and Teen Running Encyclopedia is the first ever complete guide for middle and distance runners ages 6 to 18, their coaches and parents. It shows the proven formula of Mick Grant, which produced National Champions several years in a row from a group of ordinary local kids, near Mick's home in Northeast Massachusetts. The book lays out in detail how youth and teen athletes can achieve successively higher levels, year after year after year, following the proven success of Mick's training program. What differentiates this program and this book from other programs and books is that it is a unique blend of building endurance and improving basic speed throughout the year, so that the athlete is much better next year than they are this year. The program uses a **FUN FIRST** approach, making sure the athletes enjoy what they are doing and stay healthy, to allow consistent training. It is the first such book to cover every topic imaginable for the youth and teen middle/distance runner, jammed packed with almost 200 pages of vital information. This book is a must read for all youth runners age 6 to 18, and anyone helping youth runners starting on the way to a lifelong enjoyment of running, and a successful running career. While this book is geared to youth runners, it is a valuable resource to all middle and long distance runners and coaches, regardless of age or level, because the same basic principles apply to all middle and long distance events.

Editorials and Endorsements:

Russell Brown, Professional Track & Field athlete, Nike/OTC Elite, 3:51 miler

"Mick came to me at a critical point in my athletic career. I needed to elevate the level I was competing at and needed to elevate the level I was training at accordingly. He taught me how to be the best, and what it took to win big races. He made it possible for me to receive a world-class education and work in one of the most exciting and interesting industries I can imagine, professional track & field. There are not many coaches with Mick's knowledge of the sport and commitment to the athlete, and virtually none at the youth level. He has given so much to me and to countless others during his illustrious career. I will be forever grateful."

Jerry Palazzo, Head Coach Equalizers Youth Track Club - Southern California, Jerry is considered one of if not the best youth coach in the country as his club has won 20 Junior Olympic National Team Titles and has been in the top 3 nearly 50 times.

"While reading on a subject that I consider 'my own', my opinions danced in several directions, but at the conclusion, my impression was that this book is not only comprehensive, but serves as an invaluable resource for coaches, runners, and parents of runners; and one that I'll use to make some modifications to future training regimens that I prescribe. Information on youth running is nearly non-existent, and sorely lacking; and the sport itself is questionable in many parents' minds, unlike swimming and other comparable endurance sports. The "truth" lies within this publication, in how important it is for high school and college aged runners to begin as early in life as they do so many traditional sports. Development as a runner goes far beyond what talent can bring, and the process is lengthy in order to be healthy and lasting. I highly recommend this book as a mandatory starting point."

Coach Jay Johnson, Professional Distance coach, Director of Boulder Running Camps, writer for Active.com and contributor to Running Times magazine
"Mick Grant is a fantastic coach who knows how to develop youth runners into athletes who excel at the high school level and beyond. His athletes continue to improve each year in a sport where most athletes plateau during their middle school and high school careers. I have two daughters and if they end up running I hope they have a coach as caring and capable as Mick Grant."

Dave Dyer, Eagle Tribune
"If you're looking for coaching bargains, look no further than Mick Grant of Haverhill.
As the coach of the Lynx Elite Athletics track and field club based out of Haverhill, Grant's success stories are growing at a stunning rate...
What Grant basically does is take aspiring young runners, keeps them motivated and injury-free and attempts to maximize their potential. The athletes who have run for Elite in the last few years make up a list that is like a "Who's who of New England's Young Track Superstars."

Made in the USA
Lexington, KY
17 December 2016